The Story-Teller
Retrieves the Past

THE STORY-TELLER
RETRIEVES
THE PAST

HISTORICAL FICTION AND FICTITIOUS HISTORY IN THE ART OF SCOTT, STEVENSON, KIPLING, AND SOME OTHERS

Mary Lascelles

CLARENDON PRESS · OXFORD
1980

Oxford University Press, Walton Street, Oxford OX2 6DP

OXFORD LONDON GLASGOW
NEW YORK TORONTO MELBOURNE WELLINGTON
KUALA LUMPUR SINGAPORE JAKARTA HONG KONG TOKYO
DELHI BOMBAY CALCUTTA MADRAS KARACHI
NAIROBI DAR ES SALAAM CAPE TOWN

Published in the United States by
Oxford University Press, New York

British Library Cataloguing in Publication Data

Lascelles, Mary
    The story-teller retrieves the past.
    1. Historical fiction, English — History and
    criticism
    2. English fiction — 19th century — History and
    criticism
    I. Title
    823'.081   PR830.H5   80-40186
    ISBN 0 19 812802 9

Set by Hope Services, Abingdon
and printed in Great Britain by
Billing & Sons Ltd.,
London, Guildford and Worcester

Contents

In Memory of my Father
who gave me Opportunity

Acknowledgements

To Mrs Tillotson I owe, as so often hitherto, a comprehensive debt for patient attention and wise counsel throughout the writing of this book. Without the skilful and generous help of Mrs Susan Hall, the final state would never have reached such consistency of presentation as may now be found in it. From Miss Barbara Harvey I learnt where to look for sources I needed. Mr and Mrs Emrys Jones gave me critical scrutiny and encouragement. The Librarian of the English Faculty Library and her staff eased my labours. Other, more specific, obligations are recorded in the notes.

Note on Editions and References

In default of an authoritative edition of Scott's novels and tales, I have given a reference (volume and page) to the first edition, followed by the number of the chapter as it would appear in a modern edition—with this one exception: the compact, almost elegant, volume which was published in 1827 under the designation *Chronicles of the Canongate, First Series, Volume I*, is a peculiar case. The title is not only cumbersome, but a misnomer: *The Surgeon's Daughter*, called the second volume, and *The fair Maid of Perth*, called the Second Series, are tenuously and perfunctorily attached to the Canongate and its chronicles by introductory stuff. I maintain that the volume of 1827 is the only true Canongate chronicle. It has however suffered in reprinting: in the 'Magnum' it is overloaded with an account of the occasion on which Scott publicly acknowledged his authorship of the novels; and the chapters are renumbered, inconveniently. Subsequent collected editions follow the 'Magnum', and do further damage, coupling the volume with novels to which it bears no relation, and even dismembering it and distributing the tales among several volumes. I have therefore referred to it merely as *I Canongate*, and given references to the first edition only.

For Stevenson's novels I have given the number of the chapter; for his essays, the volume in which each appeared in the first collected edition (the Edinburgh), with further information (e.g. as to date) when this mattered. For the letters, see the list of abbreviated titles. Since his wanderings are relevant, I have given the place from which each letter was written.

For Kipling's *Puck of Pook's Hill* and *Rewards and Fairies*, I have given the title of the tale and the book in which it appeared.

Abbreviated Titles of Works Frequently Referred to

Balfour, *Life*: Graham Balfour, *Life of Robert Louis Stevenson*, 2 vols. (1901).

I Canongate: Sir Walter Scott, *Chronicles of the Canongate*, First Series, Vol. I. (1827).

Grierson, *Sir Walter Scott*: H. J. C. Grierson, *Sir Walter Scott, Bart., A New Life* (1938).

James and Stevenson: *Henry James and Robert Louis Stevenson: a Record of Friendship and Criticism*, ed. Janet Adam Smith (1948).

Journal: *The Journal of Sir Walter Scott*, ed. W. E. K. Anderson (1972).

Letters, Colvin: *The Letters of Robert Louis Stevenson*, ed. Sidney Colvin, 4 vols (1911).

Letters, Grierson: *The Letters of Sir Walter Scott*, ed. H. J. C. Grierson, 12 vols. (1932–7).

Letters to Baxter: *Stevenson's Letters to Charles Baxter*, ed. Delancey Ferguson and Marshall Waingrow (1956).

Lockhart, *Life*: J. G. Lockhart, *Memoirs of Sir Walter Scott* (first published 1837–8; references to the edition of 1900, ed. A. W. Pollard, 5 vols.).

Memories of Vailima: Isobel Strong and Lloyd Osbourne, *Memories of Vailima* (1903).

Puck of Pook's Hill: Rudyard Kipling, *Puck of Pook's Hill* (1906).

Rewards and Fairies: Rudyard Kipling, *Rewards and Fairies* (1910).

Scott, *Minstrelsy*: Sir Walter Scott, *Minstrelsy of the Scottish Border*, 2 vols. (1802), 3 vols. (1803).

Introduction

Anyone who has been engaged, over long years, in teaching and writing on that fugitive subject, English literature, must have become conscious of a secret bias; an undertow, drawing interest and curiosity in a particular direction. For those of a philosophical turn of mind it will flow towards the history of ideas. For me, its destination has been the working of the imagination, alike in the story-teller and in those on whom he casts his spell. Latterly, the aim has become more precise: I wanted to know how the past challenged the imagination of both, and how that challenge was met by particular story-tellers.

It is not altogether candid to invoke authority in support of action on which we have all long been bent. Nevertheless, the countenance offered by great historians is welcome. Those of them who were not at the mercy of their political principles have always paid tribute to Scott. An ampler blessing may be inferred from Sir Richard Southern's Presidential Address to the Royal Historical Society in 1972.[1] A sense of the past, he here maintains,[2] has of late been fostered in order to heal the alienation which resulted from 'the breakdown of the relatively stable intellectual system' inherited from the Middle Ages and remaining 'substantially operative till the mid-nineteenth century'. Though former doctrines might need to be relinquished, the experiences which had given rise to them required to be preserved. 'By the imaginative appropriation of these experiences, people could still possess the past, while rejecting the intellectual structure which it had once been the role of the historical process to hand down from age to age'. But this fresh historical activity 'was not confined to historians'. Credit is given to 'non-historians', wholly imaginative writers, who

[1] 'Aspects of the European Tradition of Historical Writing, The Sense of the Past', in *Transactions of the Royal Historical Society*, Fifth Series, Vol. 23 (1973).
[2] pp. 244-5.

worked to heal the sense of alienation. This is heartening; and the developing argument offers further encouragement. 'Since history was a cure for alienation, it is not surprising that it was aliens and exiles who experienced most vividly its healing power . . . It was the returned exile Kipling—in my view the most gifted historical genius this country has ever produced—who created the most vivid imaginative pictures of the successive phases of life in England going back to a remote antiquity.' With Kipling I unhesitantly couple Robert Louis Stevenson, the exile who would not return,[3] believing that the historical insight discoverable in his writings has been overlooked. Whether those three authors of my choosing are to be regarded as witnesses to a story or companions on a journey of exploration, I thankfully acknowledge such credentials as these: Scott and Kipling commended for historical insight,[4] nothing said against Stevenson on this score.

If a book cannot justify itself, no introduction will do it, but some explanation of scope and aim may be allowed. The field being so wide, I have restricted myself to this island of Great Britain—with an inescapable bias towards Scotland: Scott and Stevenson are at their best there, and tradition and hearsay flow more strongly beyond the Border.

The choice of authors, while it went with the grain of my preference, could be justified on critical principles. Criticism is nourished by comparison, and these three are notably comparable. Not only is there a significant balance of likeness and difference; two of them may be found handling the same theme, and where this happened the way was open for a comparison with *Esmond*, though Thackeray was never at the heart of my argument.

Given such protagonists as Scott, Stevenson, and Kipling, it was hardly necessary to define historical fiction; but the reader intent on nice distinctions—to whom I am no enemy— will find a line between the historical novel and the novel

---

[3] See Lloyd Osbourne, 'Mr. Stevenson's Home Life at Vailima', in *Memories of Vailima*, pp. 77–8, and Stevenson's letters from Samoa, *passim*.

[4] See, in particular, G. M. Trevelyan, *An Autobiography and Other Essays*, (1949), and *A Layman's Love of Letters* (1954); and G. M. Young, *Scott and the Historians*, *Sir Walter Scott Lectures* (Edinburgh, 1950), also in *Last Essays* (1950).

set back in the world of the author's childhood delicately drawn in Mrs Tillotson's *Novels of the Eighteen-Forties*.[5] Another distinction, that between historical fiction and fictitious history, I attempt to draw in Chapter V.

Even supposing my choice of authors to be unexceptionable, doubt may arise as to the works chosen—so large room given to *Kidnapped*, begun as a book for boys, and Kipling confined to the *Puck* books. But *Kidnapped* outgrew its initial impulse, and Kipling's aim had always stretched beyond that first audience: the tales were to be variously understood in 'the shifting light of sex, youth, and experience.[6] They are, besides, the very tales which have been praised by historians for their insight into the past. Furthermore, one result of the Victorians' reverence for youth is that children's books are among their classics. They did not grudge their best endeavour in this field, and they practised in it an unaccustomed moderation. (Kipling was capable of exaggerating even an understatement). Here, therefore, we encounter Stevenson and Kipling in their strength, as we do Scott, in his novels of eighteenth-century Scotland.

Johnson, approaching the legendary island of Iona, reflected on the imaginative apprehension of the past: 'Whatever withdraws us from the power of our senses; whatever makes the past, the distant, or the future predominate over the present, advances us in the dignity of thinking beings.' My undertaking, then, is reputable. But the proof of a project is in the performance, and that remains to be seen.

[5] (1954), pp. 90–4.
[6] *Something of Myself*, p. 190.

Chapter I

Access to the Past

There are several ways by which the historical novelist may gain access to the past and communicate his insight to his readers. There is the written word, and the spoken word—livelier, but not able to reach so far back; and there are *things*—ruined buildings, pieces of man's handiwork once in common use. As the written word speaks to the trained mind of the historian, so these speak to the trained eye of the antiquary. But all kinds of evidence have something to say, vivid if imprecise, to the imagination. And here we must reckon, not only with the imaginative apprehension of the story-teller, but also with his reader's capacity for response. These vary from age to age, but there are certain constants to be discerned.

We must not expect any ineffaceable distinctions between these ways of approach to a past age. The story-teller may have been in practice as an historian—as Scott had been, before he wrote *Waverley*. He may throw himself into the antiquarian activities of his day—as Scott did. He will be constrained, like Scott, by contemporary assumptions as to where—in what age or place—interest is concentrated, and how curiosity can be satisfied.

There is no single or simple way of tracing Scott's course, in his approach to the past. If I can show its complexity and interest, I shall have done something. In many respects, time—the date of his birth and upbringing—were propitious; but not in all. He could count on a keen interest—at least, as to certain periods of recent history—and a more volatile, romantic curiosity as to some upland, inland region of past literature approximately defined by the scope of Percy's *Reliques*.[1] It stretched from the earliest recoverable, and intelligible, examples of English verse, to some turning-point

---

[1] The most illuminating survey of this literary territory is to be found in Arthur Johnston's *Enchanted Ground* (1964).

in the seventeenth century at which the poets began to appear to the collectors of 'ancient' poetry not altogether unlike themselves.

Much may be learnt from the answer (if you can get it) to a simple question: are you drawn to the people of a past age by a sense of likeness or difference? But for the man intent on genealogy that answer will not be simple. He is sensible of kinship with his forebears, despite the alien world in which they seem to have lived. Stevenson played with this notion, at first flippantly, then with growing seriousness and sense of purpose. He makes the relationship between Archie Weir and the elder Kirstie Elliott an occasion for this reflection: Kirstie knew 'the legend of her own family, and [might] count kinship with some illustrious dead. For that is the mark of the Scot of all classes: that he stands in an attitude towards the past unthinkable to Englishmen, and remembers and cherishes the memory of his forebears, good or bad; and there burns alive in him a sense of identity with the dead even to the twentieth generation.'[2] Leaving aside the invidious comparison, it will be enough for the present to grant the Scot's customary claim to a keen eye and tenacious memory for his own family history, and to look for its manifestation in Scott and Stevenson.

In historical, semi-historical, and fictitious writing, Scott illustrates the many paths by which it is possible to approach the past, and the way in which they turn and return upon one another like country roads. As historical novelist, he was at his best in three periods of Scottish history: the insurgence in the south-west, particularly between the murder of Archbishop Sharp and the battle of Bothwell Bridge; the '45 and its aftermath; and one phase in the long reverberations of mistrust which followed the Union of the Kingdoms. For the first he had to create an audience, at least in England; for the second he had one, captive and attentive, even in England; for the third he has never really had one, in England: *The Heart of Midlothian* is seldom read in its proper historical context.

Looking back over his career as writer of historical romance,

[2] *Weir of Hermiston*, Chapter v.3.

Scott recorded in his *Journal* some vexation at the antics of his imitators, but took comfort from the reflection: 'They may do their fooling with a better grace but I like Sir Andrew Aguecheek do it more natural. They have to read old books and consult antiquarian collections to get their information—I write because I have long since read such works and possess thanks to a strong memory the information which they have to seek for.'[3] This is manifestly true, and indeed a sizeable understatement. Scott's discovery of Percy's *Reliques* in youth makes one of the happiest passages in the Ashestiel Fragment:

As I had been from infancy devoted to legendary lore of this nature . . . it may be imagined, but cannot be described, with what delight I saw pieces of the same kind which had amused my childhood, and still continued in secret the Delilahs of my imagination, considered as the subject of sober research, grave commentary, and apt illustration, by an editor who showed his poetical genius was capable of emulating the best qualities of what his pious labour preserved.[4]

Apart from the grave literary sins at which Scott glances sympathetically under the general term 'emulation'—that is, tampering and imitating—the tradition Percy represented set too high a price on strangeness and distance: his people had to be unlike ourselves. For good or ill—and mostly for good—the magic was strong: 'The first time . . . I could scrape a few shillings together, which were not common occurrences with me, I bought unto myself a copy of these beloved volumes, nor do I believe I ever read a book half so frequently, or with half the enthusiasm.'[5] The spell did not weaken. Ten years later, Scott was writing to Charles Kirkpatrick Sharpe: 'I have Lagg's elegy[6] & am acquainted with the traditions of the period respecting most of the persecutors and persecuted saints. These traditions have in

---

[3] *Journal*, p. 214 (18 Oct. 1826).
[4] Lockhart, *Life*, I. 29–30 (under 1792).
[5] ibid., p. 30.
[6] The 'Elegy' was a lampoon on the death and future prospects of Sir Robert Grierson, 1st baronet of Lag, a notorious persecutor, and original of Sir Robert Redgauntlet in 'Wandering Willie's Tale'. He died in 1733, but the date of the 'Elegy' is uncertain. See Alexander Fergusson, *The Laird of Lag* (Edinburgh, 1886.

many cases extinguished the more early history of the Border
feuds tho' in themselves far less valuable.'[7]

This is understandable in a collector of ballads; the earlier
are often the better 'in themselves', but intrinsic merit is
not the same as value for purpose, which may depend on
what you can assimilate and put to use. It was the prose and
verse, the written and the spoken word, relating to the seventeenth and eighteenth centuries which was to provide grist
for Scott's mill. But the Percy tradition—if I may so call it
for brevity's sake—was by no means the whole story, as that
passage of recollection makes clear. Scott had learnt to listen
for echoes of the past as a child in his grandparents' home at
Sandy-Knowe. And what he heard there stuck, partly because
it had the interest and charm of family history. He learnt
from the women of the family, the guardians of tradition,
songs and ballads of Border heroes, and from the men,
accounts of the executions at Carlisle and all the bitter aftermath of Culloden.[8] These were Jacobite traditions; but Scott
told Kirkpatrick Sharpe that he was himself descended from
victims of persecution, 'for one cause or another'.[9] In the
long tragedy of Scottish history, it was possible to suffer
for King and Covenant in turn, or for neither; there was
always tribal warfare.

It should be understood that, for Scott, family history had
a wider reference than it would for his typical English counterpart; but, whereas his devotion to the idea of the clan and
the person of its head may seem strange to us, it was no alien
but a fellow Scot, James Hogg, who waited only for Scott's
death to denounce it as snobbery. Hogg had enjoyed Scott's
hospitality and benefited by his friendship. Like Henley, he
could not forgive a dead benefactor. For Scott, the house of
Buccleuch was an idea, and the reigning duke and duchess the
embodiment of that idea. Happily they—and in particular the
fourth duke, Charles, and his duchess, Harriet—deserved and
responded to this concept of their part. The impress of
this relationship can be traced in a succession of allusions,
direct and indirect. In the dowager duchess who revives and

[7] *Letters*, Grierson, I. 161; 17 Oct. 1802.
[8] Lockhart, *Life*, I. 14.
[9] *Letters*, Grierson, IV. 153; [1816].

cherishes the Last Minstrel, Scott refers directly to the first duchess, Anne, Monmouth's widow; indirectly to Harriet, Countess of Dalkeith, to whose husband, the future fourth duke, the poem is dedicated. This is made explicit when, in his Introduction to the 1830 edition, he devotes an elegiac passage to her memory. A year after the original publication of the *Lay*, Scott had explained his purpose to Surtees: his great-grandfather, Walter Scott of Raeburn, a staunch Jacobite and hero of Sandy-Knowe legend, would have suffered for his part in the '15 but for the intercession of Anne, Dowager Duchess of Monmouth and Buccleuch, 'to whom I have attempted . . . to pay a debt of gratitude'.[10] He had indeed begun to honour this obligation some years earlier, and was to continue for many more. Anne Scott, the Buccleuch heiress, had been married to James, son of Charles II and Lucy Walter. A royal bastard would not be everyone's choice of ancestor, but genealogists cannot be choosers, and Scott did his best for the Duke of Monmouth and Buccleuch. His weakness could, with the support of family papers, be extenuated; his known clemency[11] affirmed. Scott grasped every opportunity: first, in the historical introduction he wrote to the ballad of the Battle of Bothwell Bridge, when he gathered that into the third volume of the *Minstrelsy*;[12] then, in his edition of Dryden, which he had begun to plan directly after the publication of the *Lay*,[13] and completed in 1808. Here he makes *Absalom and Achitophel* the occasion for a disproportionately full and sympathetic account of Monmouth's character and career, dwelling upon his generalship at Bothwell Bridge. Moreover, the single, formal line— 'And made the charming Annabel his bride'—prompts a comparable tribute to his Duchess. Next, in *Old Mortality*, he reverts to Monmouth's part before, during, and after the battle

[10] *Letters*, Grierson, I. 342; 17 Dec. 1806. In the Ashestiel Fragment this is given as family tradition. See Lockhart, *Life*, I. 3.

[11] See David Ogg, *England in the Reign of Charles II* (1934), II. 417. He offered terms to the insurgents before the battle of Bothwell Bridge, and advocated mercy afterwards.

[12] Added in 1803. Rearrangement of the collection (after this second, enlarged edition) has obscured the original separateness of the Covenanting ballads.

[13] Grierson, *Sir Walter Scott*, p. 84.

of Bothwell Bridge and gives to his dealings with the insurgents the particularity which belongs to historical fiction,
whose heroes, whether or no they are known to history, must
be allowed to speak.[14] Last, in this train of association,
comes the account of Monmouth's characteristic but ineffectual attempts at conciliation, in *Tales of a Grandfather*.[15]
This is a work too little regarded, whether as an example of
Scott's plain English style in narrative (when he is not dis-
tracted by notions of romantic propriety), or as an indication
of his currents of thought.

Scott's mind was associative. In the verse letter to John
Marriott with which he introduced the second canto of
Marmion, he lamented the departure, supposedly temporary,
of the Duchess Harriet and her young son from Bowhill,
near Ashestiel. To Richard Heber, introducing the fourth
canto, he recalled the family legend concerning Scott of
Raeburn whom the first duchess was reputed to have saved
from the gallows. After Harriet's death in 1814—the boy had
died in 1808—there would be no more pretty allusions to
this association of the two duchesses—only the sad and
serious tribute in the Conclusion to *The Lord of the Isles*.

Walter Scott of Raeburn remained, in legendary security—
a symbol of stubborn loyalty and picturesque eccentricity.

> The simple sire could only boast
> That he was loyal to his cost;
> The banish'd race of kings revered,
> And lost his land—but kept his beard.

He had sworn not to shave it until the Stuarts were restored.[16]
Recurring thus, he illustrates a habit of mind which governed
Scott's references to the recorded past: he liked to take a
typical figure—it must be one he found in some way admirable—and come back and back to him when he wished to
recall a whole train of associations, drawn from remembered
talk or reading.

A notable example of this practice, Alexander Stewart of
Invernahyle, served for more, in Scott's historical thinking,

---

[14] Chapters xxx and xxxii.
[15] Second Series, II. 278-83; Chapters vii and viii.
[16] *Marmion*, Note 4F.

than an 'original' for the Baron of Bradwardine. To that
service his claim has been challenged: on behalf of Oliphant
of Gask,[17] and Forbes of Pitsligo.[18] This does not matter.
When Scott, in that recollective year of 1827, told Lady
Louisa Stuart 'I was always a willing listener to tales of broil
and battle and hubbub of every kind and now I look back on
it I think what a godsend I must have been while a boy to the
old Trojans of 1745 nay 1715 who used to frequent my
fathers house . . .',[19] he merely recapitulated what he had
been saying to correspondents and interlocutors over the
years. And when, continuing, he named Alexander Stewart
of Invernahyle as his 'chosen friend' among them, he rounded
off a tale told piecemeal, in talk, letters, and print, for nearly
as long.

It is possible to see Scott's depiction of Alexander Stewart
as in some sense a composite portrait, representative of all
those 'old Trojans' who haunted his imagination. Lockhart
gives a connected account of the relationship between Invernahyle and Scott, while admitting that there are areas of
doubt.[20] To do this asks simplification, and I can better show
the complexity of the problem by drawing illustrations from
a diversity of sources. There would seem to be more than one
Stewart of Internahyle. I do not of course mean this literally,
but rather in the sense that someone who has charmed our
childhood may likewise be present in the picture-gallery of
memory by reason of the part he played in a past familiar to
our elders. This is like two states of a colour-print which, in
the final impression, do not quite register.

The charmer of Scott's childhood first appears in a letter
to Robert Surtees, of 17 December 1806;[21] thereafter
frequently, always as a happy recollection—notably when
Scott tells Margaret Clephane of former Highland friends
(27 October 1809).[22] In 1824—I am giving the salient points
—Mrs Hughes of Uffington, who had corresponded with Scott

[17] Florence MacCunn, *Sir Walter Scott's Friends* (1909), p. 49.
[18] ibid., and W. S. Crockett, *The Scott Originals* (1912), pp. 18-19.
[19] *Letters*, Grierson, X. 238-9; [6] July 1827.
[20] *Life*, I. 118-20.
[21] *Letters*, Grierson, I. 342-3. I have not here taken account of Highland friends and clients of the elder Scott, who frequented the family
house but are not named.   [22] ibid., II, 263-4.

about Welsh and Highland song, visited him at Abbotsford, and recorded his talk of the 'old Jacobite chieftain'—the story of his part in the '15 and the '45, and of his plight as a fugitive after Culloden. ' "This man", said Sir W. "was the delight of my childhood—he was often at our house, and I was never out of his sight and never weary of the anecdotes which he was pleased to tell to one who, young as he was, had such pleasure in listening to him." ' These included the duel with Rob Roy and the battle of Sheriffmuir. Surely the composition of the portrait is growing bolder, the colours more distinct. Then follows the famous answer to the child's question—'I asked him how he felt before he went into action—his answer was "troth Laddie, when the bonnets were taken off to say a prayer, the guns fired and thrown away and the Claymores drawn and the pipes blawing I'd hae gien ony man a thousand merks who would have insured that I should na rin awa!" '[23] Scott recurred to the subject when they talked in London in 1826.[24] A year later comes the letter to Lady Louisa Stuart from which I have quoted that passage of retrospect. This too contains the child's question and the old man's answer, but here the battle is unnamed— merely his first experience of action—while the context is a little fuller and more circumstantial: Walter Scott, about 10 years old, is sitting on Invernahyle's knee,[25] and that would not be very long after 1779, when this 'old Trojan' was spoiling for a fight with Paul Jones.[26] But to the story in this letter there is a sad coda. 'Poor Alexander Stuart! I saw his son the other day a grog drinking half pay captain who has spent the little estate and is now an idle stupid annuitant and yet I can never help feeling kindly to him and stopping to talk to him about the memory of the high souled enthusiastic old man.'[27] It is a child's-eye view of a memorable friendship,[28] and repetition has

---

[23] Mary Anne Watts Hughes, *Letters and Recollections of Sir Walter Scott*, ed. by Horace G. Hutchinson (1904), pp. 64–5.
[24] ibid., p. 218.   [25] *Letters*, Grierson, X. 238.
[26] Mrs Hughes, p. 218, and other recollections.
[27] *Letters*, Grierson, X. 239.
[28] Lockhart is non-committal about a visit to Invernahyle in the mid-eighties; Alexander Stewart would by then have been very old—if he had indeed fought at Sheriffmuir.

not dulled the colours—indeed they glow more brightly than ever.

If we set out afresh to trace published references to this emblematic figure, the starting-point will be the first edition of *Waverley*. In 'A Postscript which should have been a Preface', Scott briefly claims historical authenticity—in general terms, and also in one particular: 'The most romantic parts of this narrative are precisely those which have a foundation in fact. The exchange of mutual protection between a Highland gentleman and an officer of rank in the king's service, together with the spirited manner in which the latter asserted his right to return the favour he had received, is literally true.'[29] Thus he signalizes the mutual good offices—*protection* is to prove a slippery word—of Edward Waverley and Colonel Talbot, in the novel. However much this terse reference is amplified, in future commentary, there will never be an admission that one of the persons in this historical transaction has been robbed to eke out the assets of the novel's titular hero.

Three years later, in that review of his own novels by which Scott hoped to preserve his anonymity, 'the late' Stewart of Invernahyle and Colonel Whitefoord are named as the two officers whose encounter at Prestonpans and its sequel afford the *romantic fact* underlying the novel. Before his public avowal of authorship in 1827, Scott, *as novelist*, was chary of mentioning names of friends and acquaintances by which he thought he might be identified, and therefore alluded obliquely to 'originals' or informants; but here he himself appears thinly disguised as a correspondent who can piece out the reviewer's incomplete knowledge of Scottish affairs. And yet the writer of the review[30] was, by the terms of the conspiracy, supposed to be William Erskine.[31] As Johnson asks, 'What is modesty if it departs from truth? Of what use is the disguise by which nothing is concealed?'[32] In 1827, after his renunciation of anonymity, Scott uttered

---

[29] III. 367, Chapter lxxii.
[30] *Quarterly Review*, XVI (Jan. 1817): *Tales of My Landlord*, pp. 430–80.
[31] Scott names him as the reviewer in *I Canongate*, p. xix. See *Note on Editions and References*, above.
[32] *Letters*, ed. R. W. Chapman (1952); Letter 49.

many of the names he had hitherto suppressed: his Introduction to the first *Chronicles of the Canongate* is explicit about the fortunes of his old friend at Prestonpans and after Culloden.[33] Finally, in the 'Magnum' *Waverley*, he recounts the story once more. In recapitulating it, I shall draw on all three versions, making particular use of that in the 1817 review, since it is at once fuller and less accessible than the other two.

When the Hanoverian troops broke and fled at Prestonpans, a single officer, Colonel Whitefoord, stood his ground. Invernahyle summoned him to surrender, and, on his refusal, succeeded in disarming him and saving him from death at the hands of a Highlander in his own following. He then persuaded him to surrender, and afterwards obtained 'from the Chevalier' freedom on parole for his prisoner. Wounded at Culloden, Invernahyle was carried home by his followers, but, his house being occupied by Cumberland's troops, he took refuge on a hillside overlooking it, where he was hidden and cared for by his servants and his 8 year-old daughter. It was now Colonel Whitefoord's turn to importune authority on Invernahyle's behalf—to no avail: there was too much against the old Jacobite. Presenting himself to the Duke of Cumberland, and meeting with yet one more refusal, 'He then limited his request for the present, to a protection for Stuart's house, wife, children, and property.' Again refused, he offered to resign his commission, upon which the Duke 'granted the protection'.[34] I quote from the 1817 version because it is the clearest on a point which may perplex readers unfamiliar with the history of those years—the distinction between protection and pardon; for his pardon, Invernahyle had to await the Act of Indemnity, and must therefore, despite his friend's success, have been a fugitive from April 1746 to June 1747.

This is a finely shaped story; and its theme, merciful exchanges between those whom civil war had made adversaries, was very close to Scott's heart. He was to return to it in *Old Mortality*, where Morton and Evandale tread a stately dance of mutual courtesies. And yet he had to spoil it. There is an odd, and (I believe) revealing error in the version of the story

[33] pp. xiii–xviii.
[34] p. 434.

which he gives in *I Canongate*: 'I may here also notice, that the sort of exchange of gallantry, which is represented as taking place betwixt the Baron of Bradwardine and Colonel Talbot, is a literal fact'.[35] Is that what is called a Freudian slip? It is silently corrected in 1831/2.[36] But of course it *should* have been the Baron of Bradwardine—and, alas, it was Edward Waverley who, sauntering on the battle-field, noticed and rescued Colonel Talbot. Everything called out for the hero of Scott's childish imagination, whose image had never faded; for the hero, in another sense—that is, the doer and sufferer—of the historical anecdote. True, he is still the sufferer, the hard-pressed fugitive—though even that will be blurred at the end. And he is restored to some degree of dignity by his sufferings: 'His absurdities, which had appeared grotesquely ludicrous during his prosperity, seemed, in the sunset of his fortune, to be harmonized and assimilated with the nobler features of his character so as to add peculiarity without exciting ridicule.'[37] But something more than the dignity of the original character was lost when Scott sacrificed the encounter of those two veterans—each in his way a professional soldier—to the claims of what he liked to call 'a connected narrative'. The Colonel Talbot who is repaying, in a contrived manner, his original debt to Sir Everard Waverley, is a mere agent of the plot, and as a character neither very plausible nor likeable. The letter in which he reports the concluding transactions to Edward Waverley is obnoxious: its flippant tone is at odds with the situation, and betrays Scott to an English style beyond his compass. Moreover, by relinquishing the Baron's cause, on the score that others have already pleaded it successfully, Talbot severs the last link with the original story; and his fluent tale of pardons and protections is no more than the froth of a conventional happy ending.

When Catherine Morland protests, in face of Isabella Thorpe's questionable behaviour, 'A woman in love with one man cannot flirt with another', Henry Tilney replies: 'It is probable that she will neither love so well, nor flirt so well, as

---

[35] p. xiii.
[36] Introduction dated 1831; published 1832, p. xviii.
[37] III. 264–5; Chapter lxv.

she might do either singly. The gentlemen must each give up a little'.[38] Scott was in love with history, but he could never resist the opportunity of a flirtation with romance—of which he was not nearly so sure a judge.

Thackeray's excursion into his own family history—as distinct from those imagined dynasties to which I shall come presently—amounts to no more than the delusion that he was descended from General Webb, and therefore owed Marlborough a grudge. It is best forgotten. Stevenson's is quite another story.

Robert Louis Stevenson was finding himself, as historical novelist, when he died. He had not of course to *find* Scottish history; it was his birthright, and a strong sense of the historical associations of familiar places had been with him from the first, as his 'Picturesque Notes on Edinburgh'[39] witness. Even a relatively late essay, 'The Coast of Fife'[40] (1888), is based on a journey he had made with his father in his thirteenth year. When he wrote it, he had behind him diligent research in Highland history, which was to have yielded a major historical work. It had so far given *Kidnapped*, and this is a tale of deliberately limited scope. It holds out promise of a wider historical vision, but some years will have to pass before that promise begins to be fulfilled. What hindered this development was (I suggest) essay-writing. This was in the first place a token of precarious health and the need for short-breathed, immediate achievement. And the form itself was an obstacle to growth in the direction of the historical novel. 'The Coast of Fife' illustrates the antagonism between these two forms: there is an air of coquetry about this 'random memory',[41] derived from a succession of writers who, throughout the nineteenth century, took Johnson's definition of the essay as 'a loose sally of the mind' all too literally. If the grammarians would but allow the term, we might say that the essay, from Charles Lamb to Virginia Woolf, is written in the evocative mood. Here, Stevenson evokes figure or incident from the recorded past only to turn away after an oblique glance. For him, Magus Muir and the

---

[38] *Northanger Abbey*, Chapter xix.
[39] Edinburgh edition, Vol. I.
[40] ibid.
[41] A subtitle he uses for several essays.

murder of Archbishop Sharp mean, not an act performed and suffered, in a given place and time, but the occasion for a flight of fanciful speculation on the enigmatic behaviour of Hackston of Rathillet, who would neither strike nor save the victim. 'Whenever I cast my eyes backward, it is to see him like a landmark on the plains of history, sitting with his cloak about his mouth, inscrutable.'[42]

I do not of course claim that the writer of historical fiction is bound to tell all, nor even to persuade us that he could if he would. On the contrary, the power of Scott's account of the Porteous riot is diminished by this very pretension: his chosen witness, Reuben Butler, does not know who the real instigator is; authority, from the humblest officer of the law to Queen Caroline herself, would give a great deal to know; but, so far as the historian[43] is concerned, a deed performed in full view of a multitude kept, and keeps, its secret. Hence its hold on the imagination. Unhappily, Scott alleges that the deviser and organizer of the affair was George Robertson; in order to carry this through, he must further pretend that his name, which belonged to a man known to history as a simple smuggler, had been assumed as an alias by the fictitious and very different George Staunton, who, in this implausible part, serves the plot and spoils the novel. Stevenson did not entangle himself in this sort of 'connected narrative'. He wisely confined his affirmation to what David Balfour saw and heard. Having himself worked over the ground of the Appin murder,[44] he maintains that, although Appin tradition is 'clear in Alan's favour', this is all you will ever discover. 'If you inquire, you may even hear that the descendants of "the other man" who fired the shot are in the country to this day. But that other man's name, inquire as you please, you shall not hear; for the Highlander values a secret for itself and for the congenial exercise of keeping it.'[45]

Whether he fairly admits default of evidence or pretends

---

[42] Edinburgh edition, Vol. I.
[43] Scott himself, in *Tales of a Grandfather*, Third Series, II. 172.
[44] See Colvin, Introduction to *Letters*, II. 5-6; and R.L.S. to his father, ibid., pp. 55-6.
[45] Dedication of *Kidnapped* to Charles Baxter.

to information beyond the historian's resources, the novelist still differs from the traditional essayist in this: it is through the consciousness of his characters that he conveys his sense of what 'really happened', so far as he chooses to make this part of his tale; whereas, for the essayist, the reverberations die at the circumference of his own consciousness.

On my reckoning, Stevenson would not be able to develop to his full stature as historical novelist until he should break free from this hampering convention of the essay. And that could not happen by a simple progression in time; essay-writing was his assured livelihood. He had an aptitude for it which must be turned to account. Talking wryly to Isobel Strong of his earlier 'honey-dropping essays', he admitted: 'I had a pretty talent that way.'[46] And he associated the talent and the taste for exercising it with youth. Maturity must await self-knowledge; and that, in such a conscious crafts-man would bring knowledge of his own latent powers. The development of these would seem to lie within Time's gift; but the giver had one hand behind his back. Self-discovery was indeed coming, but not fast enough to outstrip the forces that were destroying a precarious life. Hence the unfulfilled promise of *Weir of Hermiston*. As Johnson says, 'He that runs against Time, has an antagonist not subject to casualities.'[47]

I suggest that the nearly fulfilled promise and the self-knowledge from which it grew were, at least in part, the outcome of a slowly but steadily increasing interest in family history, and that this can be discerned in a number of circum-stances which, fortuitous as they may appear severally, together form a pattern.

Interest and pride in his forebears were not, of course, a late and sudden development. Indeed, it would have been very strange if Robert Louis Stevenson had not been proud of men who, in three generations, had ringed the deadly coast of Scotland with lighthouses, and created the service of the Northern Lights.[48] Moreover, one of them had added to his indubitably heroic qualities a vein of eccentricity. A brief reminder of the chief characters in this family saga may be

[46] *Memories of Vailima*, pp. 40-1.
[47] 'Life of Pope' (*Lives of the Poets*, ed. Birkbeck Hill, III. 117).
[48] See Craig Mair, *A Star for Seamen* (1978).

to the purpose here. In 1807 Robert Stevenson succeeded his step-father, Thomas Smith,[49] under whom he had served since the age of 19, as Engineer to the Board of Northern Lighthouses—a post to which Smith had been appointed when it, and the Board, were created, in 1786. Stevenson was in turn followed in this office, and as builder of lighthouses and improver of harbours, by three of his sons, Alan, David, and Thomas—[50] the father of Robert Louis.

It is evident that Robert Louis Stevenson had early been an attentive, and retentive, listener to his father's stories. Bright fragments are recognizable in his fiction. Jim Hawkins was not the first boy to hide in an apple barrel and hear talk not intended for him. There was in the service one Captain Soutar: an able and intrepid seaman, but something of a humbug in his approach to Robert Stevenson.

My father and uncles, with the devilish penetration of the boy, were far from being deceived; and my father, indeed, was favoured with an object-lesson not to be mistaken. He had crept one rainy night into an apple-barrel on deck, and from this place of ambush overheard Soutar and a comrade conversing in their oilskins. The smooth sycophant of the cabin had wholly disappeared, and the boy listened with wonder to a vulgar and truculent ruffian.[51]

Kidnapped affords an illustration less obvious but still worth considering. When David asks Alan how he escaped from the infuriated seamen after the wreck of the brig *Covenant*, he replies: 'I set my best foot forward, and whenever I met with anyone I cried out there was a wreck ashore.'[52] And that disposed at one stroke of the survivors of the crew and his enemies in the Campbell-held region. That the dwellers along the Scottish coast had been wreckers would not be unknown to nineteenth-century readers, but the grim succinctness of that allusion suggests something more than common knowledge, and may reflect an image imprinted on Stevenson's

[49] Grandfather, by the marriage between his daughter and Robert, to Robert's sons.
[50] Alan 1807–65; David 1815–86; Thomas 1818–87. Alan was Engineer to the Board from 1843; David and Thomas jointly from 1853.
[51] *Records of a Family of Engineers* (1912), pp. 57–8.
[52] Chapter xviii.

mind by a particular occurrence—one which 'I have been in
the habit of hearing related by an eye-witness, my own
father, from the earliest days of childhood'. Serving under *his*
father, young Thomas Stevenson had narrowly escaped death
when their ship, the *Regent*, driven onto a lee shore, fired a
distress signal—and the whole population of the village to
which this appeal was directed turned out to await the spoils,
when she should go down before their eyes. A change of
wind saved her, but the grown man never forgot how, as a
boy, he had been regarded as their natural prey by boys of
his own age.[53]

It appears that the impulse to gather and preserve such
records began with the death of Thomas Stevenson on 8 May
1887. His son wrote a brief but poignant memoir, which
appeared next month in the *Contemporary Review*, and was
reprinted in that same year in *Memories and Portraits*. There
is other prompting, here, besides natural piety, though that
works strongly: Stevenson indeed held that his father was
undervalued outside his own professional world; but there is
something more underlying the decent reticence of these
words: 'before the clouds began to settle on his mind'.[54]
That mind gave way altogether at the end. What this meant
to the only son, who had been estranged and reconciled, is
reflected in the verse fragment beginning 'Once more I saw
him'.[55] It tells of the moment when 'the dread changeling',
that mere simulacrum of his father, failed to recognize him.
A letter to Colvin of that June expresses thankfulness that
this 'suffering changeling' is now at rest, and the hope that
'He will begin to return to us in the course of time, as he was
and as we loved him'.[56] In his own last year, Stevenson,
writing to comfort his friend Adelaide Boodle in her loss,
reminded her of the assurance she had given in his: 'You
told me those ugly images of sickness, decline, and impaired
reason, which then haunted me day and night, would pass

[53] *Records of a Family of Engineers*, pp. 54–5.
[54] *Thomas Stevenson: Civil Engineer*, Edinburgh edition, Vol. I.
[55] Robert Louis Stevenson, *Collected Poems*, ed. Janet Adam Smith,
p. 282. Omitted by Colvin from the Edinburgh edition. Whatever the
date of composition, the poem evidently refers (as this editor affirms)
to the death of Thomas Stevenson.
[56] *Letters*, Colvin, II. 322; from Edinburgh.

away and be succeeded by things more happily characteristic.'[57] And so they had. Surely he had done much
towards the achievement of this by the task he had set
himself in 1888, when he wrote to his father's friend, Dr
Charteris: 'If . . . you should recall something memorable
of your friend, his son will heartily thank you for a note
of it.'[58] This in itself implies no commitment to action
on his part. Within a month or two, however, he was writing
to ask Thomas Mowbray for family papers.[59] According
to Graham Balfour, Stevenson long contemplated the writing
of a family history, as the 'frame' for 'a memorial of his
father', but began working on it only in the summer of
1891[60]—a delay which the conditions of his life in the
preceding three years would explain. From that time until
the end references to the work occur so frequently in
his letters that I can give no more than a chosen few, and
try to indicate the direction in which the project was
developing.

Two generalizations seem appropriate here: the work
was taken up from time to time as a relaxation from the
more arduous demands of fiction; and, even in those last
years when Isobel Strong was his amanuensis for private
correspondence as well as work intended for publication,
these notes and drafts seem to have been in his own hand.

Whatever the initial impetus or design, it looks as though
Robert Stevenson had quickly taken over. He had clear
advantages, as a subject: he had died before his grandson
was born—there would be no personal anguish in the writing;
he had however left behind him not only a vivid family
legend, but also a quantity of writing, published and unpublished. He had known extremes of fortune; had been
acquainted with famous men—his association with Walter
Scott came into the story; above all, he was at the same
time indubitably heroic, and comic—'He was a fine old

---

[57] ibid., IV. 279; from Vailima, 14 July 1894.
[58] ibid., III. 47; from Saranac Lake, winter 1887–8.
[59] Enclosure in a letter to Charles Baxter. *Letters to Baxter*, p. 188;
from Saranac Lake, 26 Feb. 1888.
[60] *Life*, II. 137. There are references, in the correspondence of the
following years, to three of the 'family of engineers', but I have found
none to David.

fellow, but a droll.'[61] Already by summer 1891, when a settled home enables him to work on this material, Robert Louis Stevenson is offering to Burlingame, the editor of *Scribner's Magazine*, his grandfather's reminiscences of the famous 'lighthouse voyage' with Walter Scott. This 'may forestall one of the interests of my biography', but, with some small omissions, seems to him suitable for independent publication.[62] Although Robert Stevenson had written down these recollections at the very end of his life, with memory faltering, their interest as a complement to Scott's own diary[63] has been recognized, and something more might be claimed on the score of merit. For the purpose of my present argument, however, it is his grandson's brief introduction that matters.[64] It shows how far forward he already was, with that 'biography'. The portrait of the old man is almost complete. The climax, his approach to death, should be familiar from the passage quoted by Graham Balfour.[65] At this stage, his grandson could well have completed and published a memoir, comparable with that of Fleeming Jenkin (1888), and prefixed it to Robert Stevenson's account of his building of the Bell Rock Lighthouse. But he was intent on something of larger scope. By September, the plans for a family chronicle are drawn out: it is now 'my *Lives of the Stevensons*' (though the title of the published work has still to be determined), and, with one notable exception, corresponds with the fragment drafted by 1893, so far as that goes. Here is the scheme sent to Colvin from Vailima in September 1891: 'Chapter I. Domestic Annals. Chapter II. The Northern Lights. Chapter III. The Bell Rock. Chapter IV. A Family of Boys. Chapter V. The Grandfather. VI. Alan Stevenson. VII. Thomas Stevenson'.[66] Of these, we possess the first three chapters named in the scheme, together with an Introduction. This, called 'The Surname of Stevenson,' is a search for ancestors. Genealogical enquiry is a congenial Scottish ploy; for a Scot in exile it becomes a passion. This

[61] *Letters*, Colvin, III. 286; to Colvin from Vailima, Sept. 1891.
[62] ibid., p. 274.
[63] Lockhart, *Life*, II. 338–463.
[64] *Scribner's Magazine*, New York, XIV. (Oct. 1893), 493–502.
[65] *Life*, I. 7–8.
[66] *Letters*, Colvin, III. 283; from Vailima, Sept. 1891.

substantial fragment was included in the first collected edition (the Edinburgh), and in subsequent complete collections. It was printed separately in 1912.[67] *The Manuscripts of R. L. Stevenson's Records of a Family of Engineers*, edited by J. C. Bay,[68] is a collection of papers relating to this work: drafts of parts of further chapters, sometimes in more than one state, family letters, and information from William Swan, first cousin and adviser of Thomas Stevenson. Graham Balfour had carried home with him the part of the work completed by August 1893, to be delivered to Colvin and set up in type for convenience of revision.[69] Conjectures about possible ancestry had been submitted to J. S. Stevenson, a distant cousin and genealogist,[70] and found to need correction; but, the author being dead when the fragment was published, the text had to stand, with a caveat.

Graham Balfour made judicious use of this essay in family history, in the opening chapters of his *Life*. My concern is with the insight into the past which his work on it engendered in Stevenson.[71] Nevertheless, believing the *Family of Engineers* to be undeservedly neglected, I offer two brief illustrations of the quality of the writing, even in the questionable Introduction: by means of legal records, 'we are able to trace the existence of many other and more inglorious Stevensons, picking a private way through the brawl that makes Scots history'—and this: 'On the whole, the Stevensons may be described as decent, reputable folk, following honest trades—millers, maltsters, and doctors, playing the character parts in the Waverley Novels with propriety, if without distinction.'[72]

A few quotations from Stevenson's letters over these years may serve to illustrate the degree to which work on family records wove itself into his thought and imagination. He tells Colvin that he is pleased with what he has written on his grandfather—though it may need a fourth revision—but

---

[67] This is the edition I have used for reference.
[68] Chicago, 1929.
[69] *Letters*, Colvin, IV. 211; to Colvin from Vailima, and Colvin's note in the Edinburgh edition, Vol. XVIII; also Edmund Gosse's bibliographical note in the Pentland edition, Vol. XV.
[70] *Letters*, Colvin, IV. 197; from Vailima, 19 June 1893.
[71] See Chapter iii, pp. 79-82, below.
[72] *Records of a Family of Engineers*, pp. 2 and 7.

baffled by the problems of his father's life and that of his uncle Alan, and hampered by want of books—'Lord! if I were among libraries.'[73] Satisfaction in his grandfather as *subject* continues, but he is to find that there is too much material for this part of the work.[74] Then again, he delights in biography, and considers it less taxing than fiction,[75] but presently the problem of arrangement in this intricate family chronicle begins to tease him.[76] Two references to the significance he found in the work demand to be quoted here—one of them from this same letter: 'I have a strange feeling of responsibility, as if I had my ancestors' *souls* in my charge, and might miscarry with them.' The other passage comes even closer to *Weir of Hermiston*: 'I wish to trace my ancestors a thousand years, if I trace them by gallowses. It is not love, not pride, not admiration; it is an expansion of the identity, intimately pleasing, and wholly uncritical; I can expend myself in the person of an inglorious ancestor with perfect comfort: or a disgraced, if I could find one.'[77]

The writer of historical fiction—that is, the writer who offers us a vision of the past, drawn from history (or what men have believed to be history) and amplified by imagination—stands, no matter whether he uses narrative or dramatic form, in a peculiar relation to his reader. We need not here reckon with the audience at a play: the dramatist has, so to speak, two ports of call, and it is at the second, where he meets the reader of his printed text, that this consideration arises. By the nature of his undertaking, the story-teller who draws on history impels us to ask what he has been reading in the course of his search for access to the past. Whereas other works of imagination may perhaps allow us to speculate on their several sources of inspiration, and the scavenging critic to talk, sometimes plausibly, of personal experience or plagiarism, he alone enjoins on us the pursuit of this enquiry: with what historical documents was he acquainted, when he

[73] *Letters*, Colvin, IV. 176-7; from Vailima, 17 June 1893.

[74] *James and Stevenson*, pp. 225-6; from Vailima, 17 June 1893; and *Letters to Baxter*, p. 336, [from Vailima, 19 July 1893].

[75] *Letters*, Colvin, IV. 181; to Gosse [from Vailima], 18 June 1893.

[76] ibid., p. 201; to Colvin [from Vailima], Aug. 1893.

[77] *Letters*, Colvin, IV. 266; to R. A. M. Stevenson [from Vailima, 17 June 1894].

reached backwards beyond memory—his own or his elders'—
and outside family tradition?

There have been investigations, extensive if not conclusive,
into this documentary stuff. On the one hand, there stands
that altar of scholarship and criticism to which every succeeding generation has brought its own offerings—proposed
'sources' for Shakespeare's history plays. To this accumula-
tion we may all contribute—indeed, we cannot help it, since
every age must gather fresh matter for consideration, some of
it relevant.[78] But such a process of accretion is liable to
create a Shakespeare at work among documents filed by
well-trained assistants. These are the dreams of a lexicographer
doomed to wake a poet. On the other hand, we may be
offered guidance, drawn from a novelist's private papers,
through a prescribed stretch of past time: the record of
Thackeray's reading for *Esmond*.[79] This I mean to leave on
one side, pleading that no further labour is needed. Moreover,
the most carefully documented part of the story belongs to
Esmond's foreign campaigns, and I deal with happenings on
English or Scottish soil.

What then remains to be done? We have still to consider
particular evidence as to the means and method of access
to written history, which have been overlooked, like Stevenson's, or overlaid with miscellaneous citation, like Scott's.

Sheer quantity of information obscures our view of Scott
as historian. By far the greater part of our knowledge, or
half-knowledge, of his sources derives from Scott himself,
but erratically, capriciously, even mischievously. In the
interest of his fancied anonymity, he suppressed the names
of those who had furnished matter for his novels, and even
lied to them, denying his authorship of *Waverley* in a letter
to Miss Clephane,[80] and of *Old Mortality* to Joseph Train.[81]
Acknowledgement is likewise governed by other considerations than plain truth: Joseph Train is handsomely thanked
for his help, in the notes to *The Lord of the Isles* on its

[78] For example, Emrys Jones's *The Origins of Shakespeare* (1977).

[79] See J. A. Sutherland, *Thackeray at Work* (1974); also his edition
of *Esmond* (1970).

[80] *Letters*, Grierson, III. 512; 29 Oct. 1814.

[81] ibid., IV. 323; 21 Dec. 1816.

first appearance,[82] but for any mention of his diligence in the service of the novels he must wait for the 'Magnum' edition.[83] And by this time Scott is writing under such cruel pressure that annotation is uncertainly distributed.[84] There had, it is true, always been idiosyncrasy in his allocation of notes, The verse romances carry more, from the beginning, than the novels were ever to do, and the flimsiest among them, *The Lord of the Isles*, nearly sinks under its load of geographical, genealogical, and historical documentation—from which we may infer that the story promised by its title is a mere pretext for that other whose culmination is Bannockburn.

In this welter of evidence it should prove worth while to trace a single vein in Scott's working of written sources, one which illustrates his sustained scrutiny, over many years, of men and matters to be apprehended through the written word. For the '45 he had been able to rely on ample resources of the spoken word. Indeed, he was so well furnished with the recollections of those engaged on both sides that he could have turned round and given a lively account of the situation in Edinburgh from the whig point of view, drawing on remembered talk of Henry Mackenzie, John Home, and Alexander Carlyle.[85] But, when Lockhart distinguishes *Old Mortality* as a *first* attempt to write an historical novel from 'material furnished by books', he is inadvertently telling a half-truth. Indubitably there is a contrast between Scott's reliance in *Waverley* on the 'narratives of his *Invernahyles*', and the reading required for *Old Mortality*; and he knew it. His letters, as Lockhart observes, written during its progress, 'represent him as strong in the confidence that the

---

[82] A note on Canto V, stanza xvii in 1815 attributes the legend of the mysterious signal light to Train, and mentions his *Poems, illustrative of Many Traditions in Galloway and Ayrshire.*

[83] He is thanked in the introduction to the 1830 edition of *Old Mortality*, and in Note xvi in *The Heart of Midlothian* (in the same year). For his usefulness to Scott, see Lockhart's *Life* and John Patterson, *Memoir of Joseph Train* (1857).

[84] Having lavished notes on the Covenanters in *Old Mortality*, he found himself impoverished when he came to Wandering Willie's Tale in *Redgauntlet.*

[85] See, for example, his review of Mackenzie's *Life and Works of the Author of Douglas* for the *Quarterly* (June 1827).

industry with which he had pored over a library of forgotten tracts would enable him to identify himself with the time in which they had birth' as wholeheartedly as though he had listened to the actors and eye-witnesses of those events.[86] This is epitomized in a letter to Lady Louisa Stuart of 14 November 1816; from confidence in his subject he passes to reliance on his own readiness to handle it: 'I am complete master of the whole history of these strange times both of persecutors & persecuted so I trust I have come decently off.'[87] True; but the innovation which Lockhart claims is merely that part of the truth which shows above ground, this very letter being a counterpart of one he had written to Sharpe in 1802.[88] It has not been sufficiently noticed how continuously and strongly the line runs from the *Minstrelsy* to *Old Mortality*, and beyond that again to *Tales of a Grandfather*.

Scott could not grow up when and where he did without considerable knowledge of the Covenanters; but he was not reared in the terrible consciousness of their history which Stevenson suffered under the dominion of his devoted nurse. Knowledge and the desire to know more seem to have originated with his work for the third volume of the *Minstrelsy*. Those who are familiar with this work only in later editions than the first, whether in three volumes or one, cannot easily appreciate the separateness of that third volume, added in 1803, or its strong coherence, obscured by later dispersal of the material. In its original form, it inspired Scott to write a continuous historical narrative of the turbulence among the south-western Whigs, and his absorption in this undertaking is reflected in his letters of 1802 and 1803.[89] Although he would presently apologize to Anna Seward for the crudity of the covenanting ballads,[90] he never lost interest in the historical situation they reflected. The enjoyment which he had shared with Sharpe, Hogg, and Laidlaw still glowed in that letter from which I have already quoted,

---

[86] *Life*, III. 84-5.   [87] *Letters*, Grierson, IV. 291-5.
[88] See p. 3, above.
[89] See, for example, *Letters*, Grierson, I. 141-2, 152-4, 161, 169-71.
[90] ibid., pp. 179-82.

written to Lady Louisa Stuart when he was deep in *Old Mortality*:

It is a covenanting story the time lies at the era of Bothwell Brigg the scene in Lanarkshire: there are noble subjects for narrative during that period full of the strongest light & shadow, all human passions stirr'd up & stimulated by the most powerful motives, & the contending parties as distinctly contrasted in manners & in modes of thinking as in political principles.

From his discovery of the covenanting ballads onwards, Bothwell Bridge is Scott's Shrewsbury. It makes that adventitious appearance in his Dryden to which I have referred. Not only is it the true climax of *Old Mortality*; it becomes a point of reference, a means of measuring distance in time, and much besides. Bailie Nicol Jarvie recalls how his father the deacon—whose appearances in *Rob Roy*, though posthumous, project a shadow—fought at 'Bothwell Brig'.[91] Davie Deans's involvement with the insurgents is intrinsic to the story of *The Heart of Midlothian*, and must be considered in that context.[92] The reputation of Sir Robert Grierson of Lagg furnishes the situation and sets the tone of Wandering Willie's Tale in *Redgauntlet*, though Scott has to play fast and loose with Redgauntlet family history to reach so far back into the seventeenth century. His vision of these events is still fresh and strong in *Tales of a Grandfather*: not only were they full of the contrasted colours to which his mind's eye responded; they were documented in the way he had always liked. As he had preferred romantic chronicle to historical assessment for the verse romances, so he turned to memoirs, tracts, and pamphlets for the novels.[93]

Stevenson's discovery of the past cannot be traced in the same way, and yet there are significant resemblances. Scott delighted in making the reader acquainted with his sources; he wrote to Miss Hayman: 'I am just now finishing my romantic poem of Marmion a tale of war & wonder with notes like Noah's ark an ample receptacle for every thing that

---

[91] II. 284-5; Chapter xxvi.
[92] See Chapter IV below.
[93] e.g. John Howie, Patrick Walker, Robert Wodrow.

savours of romantic lore.'[94] He had learnt how to deploy his
resources in the *Minstrelsy*, especially that third volume. He
would not be able to make free use of this practice in the
novels until he came to acknowledge them, but the Magnum
volumes are loaded—sometimes overloaded—with extracts
from more or less relevant documents. Stevenson twice gave
an account of the genesis of stories set in a past age: *Treasure
Island* and *The Master of Ballantrae*. But both are wrapped in
the tissue paper of the essay, and are—perhaps for that reason
—introspective. When his friends planned the Edinburgh
edition, Sidney Colvin wrote to Charles Baxter: 'As to the
query about explanatory prefaces, for God's sake let there be
none of them. Strictly historical notes to *David Balfour* by
all means . . . ', but he deprecates such another exposure
as that of *Treasure Island*.[95] Stevenson had told Baxter
of those two prefaces, one already written, that on *The
Master of Ballantrae* drafted, and had admitted reluctantly
'I suppose an historical introduction to *David Balfour* is
unavoidable.'[96] He does not explain this reluctance, and it
cannot have been want of material, though that material may
no longer have been readily available. It had been ample, as
early letters witness.

Here a wide divergence between Scott and Stevenson
becomes apparent. Scott had not to ask for books. Stevenson,
whether at Davos, in America, or on Samoa, must write for
one and another—and perhaps the first again. Travel, and the
vicissitudes of health that made it necessary, compelled him
to rely on family and friends. This cuts both ways: we have,
as it were, the story of his reading—what he read and what
he meant to read—with a fulness to which there is no counterpart in Scott's correspondence—nor in any other, so far
as I know. On the other hand, this narrative line is broken,
or fades from view, as these mischances force him to abandon
a plan, or set it aside in the hope of future recovery. There is,
for example, the Highland history he was to have written
with his father.[97] Then his interest concentrates and settles

[94] *Letters*, Grierson, I. 393; 10 Nov. [1807].
[95] *Letters to Baxter*, pp. 346-7; [7 Feb. 1894].
[96] ibid., p. 344; from Vailima, 1 Jan. 1894.
[97] e.g. *Letters*, Colvin, II. 12-13; to his father from Davos, [12 Dec.

on the tale of the Forfeited Estates and the Appin murder.
Here continuity persists, however faintly. Whereas the Highland history had receded from view, only to re-emerge when
he came to teach Isobel Strong's child Scottish history at
Vailima,[98] the line of Stevenson's interest in the Appin
murder and its cause runs ineffaceably through fourteen of
his few years. It is, as might be expected, an episode in
the Highland history. Later in that same year, Stevenson
calls it 'the beautiful story of the tenants on the Forfeited
Estates'[99]—this, recounted by Alan Breck, was to move even
the sceptical David Balfour.[100] And, at the end of 1894,
he is writing to Charles Baxter: 'I say, should I not subscribe
to the Scottish History Society? I am greatly taken with one
I see referred to as being in the Press: *The Forfeited Estates
Papers, 1745-6*. How are these books sold? If I have to join
in order to get them, why I'll join.'[101] He would hardly need
them even for the most elaborate historical notes on *Catriona*;
he had long possessed an account of the trial of James
Stewart for the Appin murder.[102] Surely this request points
to an abiding interest in what lay behind those events.

Until he came to *Weir of Hermiston*, Stevenson had to
rely on the written word to open the past to him. The tenor
of those documents for which he asked shows him converging
on the way which Scott had always followed: almost all are
legal. That was to be expected while he was engaged on the
Appin case; no need to explain his absorption in 'that blessed
little volume my father bought for me in Inverness in the
year of grace '81, I believe—the trial of James Stewart, with
the Jacobite pamphlet and dying speech appended . . . '.[103]
But as he works on family tradition a sense of the wider
implications of legal history grows in him: '. . . the law . . .
acts as a kind of dredge, and with dispassionate impartiality

---

1880]. Subsequent references may be traced through Colvin's index
and commentary.

[98] *Letters*, Colvin, III. 306; to Colvin from Vailima, Oct.-Nov. 1891.
[99] ibid., II. 21; to Colvin from Davos, [Christmas 1880].
[100] *Kidnapped*, Chaper xii.
[101] *Letters to Baxter*, p. 371; [from Samoa, 16 Apr. 1893].
[102] *Letters*, Colvin, II. 56; to Thomas Stevenson [from Davos,
Oct. 1893].
[103] ibid., IV. 214; to Colvin [from Vailima], Aug.-Sept. 1893.

brings up into the light of day, and shows us for a moment, in the jury-box or on the gallows, the creeping things of the past.'[104] Scott would have concurred.

There are two reasons for this agreement, and one lies on the surface: both men were bred to the law. They were not daunted by legal records; they knew how to make use of them, and found nourishment where others would see only husks. Stevenson tells Henry James: 'Fountainhall[105] is prime, two big folio volumes, and all dreary, and all true, and all as terse as an obituary; and about one interesting fact on an average in twenty pages, and ten of them unintelligible for technicalities. There's literature, if you like! It feeds; it falls about you genuine like rain.'[106] This, of course, is humorous exaggeration, a pleasantry addressed to one who will certainly not read 'Fountainhall'. A request to Baxter had conveyed his real appreciation: 'How about my old friend Fountainhall's *Decisions*? I remember as a boy that there was some good reading there':[107] and he goes on to ask for a loan of this and other, similar records. He was working on *Weir of Hermiston*, which would, in the event, raise difficult points of law, but for the present was seeking, not solutions to particular questions, but sustenance. Scott, when he piled the Porteous papers into the 'Magnum' *Heart of Midlothian*, seems to have expected the reader to digest them raw.

Something deeper underlies this professional interest. G. M. Young, speaking on 'Scott and the Historians', made this claim: to what he has gathered in his Liddesdale raids, Scott brings 'the mind of a lawyer interested not so much in the higher branches of his science as in the human spectacle which is for ever unrolling before the lawyer's eye, and which it is the business of the lawyer to reduce to order'.[108]

---

[104] *Records of a Family of Engineers*, p. 2.

[105] Sir John Lauder, Lord Fountainhall, *The Decisions of the Lords of Council and session from June 6th, 1678, to June 30th, 1721* (Edinburgh, 1759–61).

[106] *James and Stevenson*, pp. 232–3; Stevenson to James, from Apia, July 1893.

[107] *Letters to Baxter*, p. 327; [from Samoa, 16 Apr. 1893].

[108] *Sir Walter Scott Lectures 1940–48* (Edinburgh 1950, p. 94. This lecture was delivered in 1946 and is printed also in his *Last Essays* (1950).

In the mediaeval world, however, he finds Scott at a disadvantage in comparison with the modern historian, methods
of interpretation having so far advanced, between his day and
ours, that it is now possible to say: though nothing of importance may have happened in such a place, at such a time,
' "People were talking. Let us stop and listen." '[109] But
His illustrations, alike actual and imagined, give the answer:
this talk is about a point of law, and, when that is the issue,
the spoken word is likely to have been recorded and preserved.[110]

It now becomes apparent that the convenient but arbitrary
line of division which I proposed to draw between the
written and the spoken word, as source of information for
historical fiction, must sometimes be straddled. Though
Stevenson could not listen to the talk of the 1790s as Scott
listened to that of the survivors from the '45, he knew what
Lord Braxfield had said.[111]

Kipling's means and method of access to the past require
a very different sort of consideration. Such account of them
as he gives in *Something of Myself* is designed to tease. Where
he does volunteer information about this historical insight,
it tends to specify things rather than books. Nevertheless
he allows the power of words to be understood; and, distance in time precluding the spoken word—none of his
tales in this kind comes within reach of memory—and circumstances affording no family papers, he obliges us to speculate
on the books at his disposal, and the use he made of them. At
the heart of such speculation stands the question: what does
he mean us to infer from that passage lamenting the historical
novel he never wrote?

Yet I dreamed for many years of building a veritable
three-decker out of chosen and long-stored timber—teak,
green-heart, and ten-year-old oak knees—each curve melting
deliciously into the next that the sea might nowhere meet
resistance or weakness; the whole suggesting motion even

---

[109] ibid., p. 94.
[110] For witness to this, see such collections as *The Oxford Book of
English Talk*, ed. James Sutherland (1953).
[111] *Records of a Family of Engineers*, p. 18. This could, however,
derive from Edinburgh tradition.

when, her great sails for the moment furled, she lay in some needed haven—a vessel ballasted on ingots of pure research and knowledge, roomy, fitted with delicate cabinet work below decks, painted, carved, gilt and wreathed the length of her, from her blazing stern-galleries outlined by bronzy palm-trunks, to her rampant figurehead—an East Indiaman worthy to lie alongside *The Cloister and the Hearth*.[112]

It would be barbarous to quote less than the whole of that sentence, but our challenge and search for the meaning should be aimed at two phrases: 'ballasted on ingots of pure research and knowledge', and 'worthy to lie alongside *The Cloister and the Hearth*'. When an almost oppressively clever writer pays such a tribute to one simpler than himself, we are impelled to weigh it in the scales of conjecture. One particular story (I believe) allows us to assay those ingots.

In 'Simple Simon'[113] the children learn from a companion of Sir Francis Drake's youth about his early years, how he acquired his skill in navigation and found his vocation. Simon Cheyneys tells them that he was with Drake ' "In the fetchin' trade" ', and explains what this meant: ' "Fetchin' poor Flemishers and Dutchmen out o' the Low Countries to England" '—rescuing fugitives from Spanish oppression. Presently he recalls how, when they were in Rye Harbour, his aunt, who ' "had gifts by inheritance laid up in her" ', came on board, and Drake coaxed her to read his hand. She foretold the great voyage of circumnavigation, and what it would mean to him. Simon's devotion is lifelong, but, being wounded in a skirmish with a Spaniard ' "next time we slipped out for some fetchin' trade" ', he sees no more of Drake until, twenty years later, he is able, as a ship-builder, to bring him sorely needed supplies in the fight with the Armada. Into this tale is woven one of Kipling's favourite themes: the untimely birth of an invention or discovery. Simon has his own visionary gifts: he dreams of iron ships, but must forgo work on them, since it is wooden walls that England needs. This is, even by Kipling's standards, a subtly constructed story.

I cannot learn, even with generous help from historians,[114]

[112] *Something of Myself*, p. 228.   [113] *Rewards and Fairies*.
[114] Especially Professor John Bromley and Mr Alastair Duke.

that there is any foundation for this assertion of Drake's part in the escape of refugees from the Netherlands—which was happening in the 1560s. Is the tale then to be regarded simply as one of those historical events that never happened[115]—an airy fabric of actions attributed to historical characters, but many of them going clean against the record of history? I offer an alternative suggestion.

If we take into account books which could well have come Kipling's way from boyhood onwards, we shall get no more than this brief account of the years before Drake became famous—that is, before his first Atlantic voyage: he was apprenticed to the skipper of a small coasting vessel, trading along the English shore of the Straits of Dover, and occasionally—for she was only just sea-worthy—crossing to the Low Countries and France. He commended himself to his master who, dying childless, bequeathed the vessel to him; and for a while he continued to trade in her. Of those books which carry the story forward from this slender beginning—originating with Camden—three would surely be available to Kipling, and seem to have furnished matter for that far inferior tale, 'Gloriana': the standard biography, John Barrow's *The Voyages and Explorations of Admiral Sir Francis Drake* (1843), the standard historical account of the Low Countries in those years, J. L. Motley's *History of the United Netherlands*, of which I have used the four-volume edition of 1869; and, later but still in good time, Julian Corbett's *Drake and the Tudor Navy*—I have used the two-volume edition of 1899. To these I add conjecturally, since Kipling was of an enquiring mind and enjoyed the freedom of two private libraries while still at school,[116] Thomas Fuller's *The Holy and the Profane State*—to which foot-notes in those others would send him, and of which an unpretentious edition appeared in 1840. The idea of a connection between Drake and the Protestant refugees would be so congenial to these four writers that we may be sure, if a trace of it were to be found in their sources, they would have mentioned it, with whatever reservation. They do not. And yet it may be claimed that, if they give no warrant for the belief, they leave room for a surmise.

[115] See Chapter V, below.　　　[116] *Something of Myself*, p. 36.

Motley arrests attention with a passage—remarkable because undocumented—about Drake as the Queen's emissary to the Netherlands in 1586; observes that this was 'not the first time that he had visited' this country, and recalls his voyages in 'the small lugger which traded between the English coast and the ports of Zeeland'[117] when, according to Fuller, 'he underwent a hard service; and pains with patience did knit the joints of his soul, and made them more solid and compacted'.[118] Moreover, he includes in 'the profane state'—that is, among the damned—the notorious Duke of Alva, whose cruelties drove the Netherlanders to take refuge in England.[119] Corbett clinches the point when he attributes Drake's pugnacious Protestantism to early experience: he was 'by his calling brought into contact with Alva's inhuman persecutions across the sea'.[120] Singly, these passages could refer to the hazards of trading in those waters. Even in conjunction they hardly amount to an invitation to suppose that Drake was engaged in anything more dangerous than ordinary trade. But the force of an invitation consists in our readiness to accept, and Kipling would find in a complete and circumstantial life, such as Barrow's, something to prompt acceptance. When Drake emerges into the unsparing light of history, it is as a slave-trader. Barrow's plea that this was in accord not only with the practice but even with the moral theory of his age is fair historical perspective; but it will not do for a story told to children. So, reaching back beyond the slave-trading of 1567, into the unrecorded years, Kipling turns the least hint to account, and fills the dark interstice with the appropriate event. This, unlike the one that could never have happened, contains both as to character and situation an element of probability. On what other terms would Drake be trading with territory we should now describe as 'occupied'? But where are the 'ingots of research'? Can Kipling have hoped that, somewhere among unpublished papers, the evidence for what he had *supposed* might lie *perdu*?[121]

---

[117] I. 95.

[118] (1840), p. 107.

[119] ibid., p. 397.

[120] I. 71.

[121] —as had the evidence for a Roman legion's service on the Wall. See *Something of Myself*, p. 189. That evidence, however, has latterly been challenged. See A. L. F. Rivet, 'Rudyard Kipling's Roman Britain' (*Kipling Journal*, June 1978), pp. 6-8.

The biographer, the literary historian, and (I surmise) the historian proper, must sometimes proceed by verifying intuition. But intuition is a function of the imagination, and a quick imagination will not easily be persuaded to wait on the slow process of verification. Moreover, the intuitive apprehension is not inseparable from the wish to believe—to be assured, for example, of the merit of the chosen subject. Hence the hero of play or novel, though known to history, may be credited with deeds which, though unknown to history, are within the scope of the character attributed to him: More may intercede on behalf of the 'aliens'—characteristically, but in an improbable situation; Drake may rescue fugitives from persecution, in a likely situation and with characteristic daring.[122]

If I have seemed to dwell inordinately on this one tale, it is because Kipling's handling of his sources in 'Simple Simon', together with his appreciation of Charles Reade's assiduity, may help us to define the obligation of the writer of historical fiction to recorded history.

---

[122] That difference between the two situations compels me to defer Shakespeare's part in the play of *Sir Thomas More* until a later chapter. See pp. 122-128, below.

Chapter II

A Sense of the Past

Somewhere beyond this deployment of the spoken and the written word, whether systematic or capricious, and a little way short of historical insight, there is a force to be reckoned with: the sense of the past. It draws on wider and more various sources than the first; it is distinguished from the second by its reliance on the reader's response. No documentation, however thorough, will make this factor unnecessary; nor will a lively pictorial imagination take its place. It stretches, an invisible but indispensable web of connection, between writer and reader. It will sometimes correspond with, sometimes diverge from, the sense of history.

This power does not merely mean an ability for establishing imaginary characters in a world which existed some while ago. They will be only the figures of familiar fiction in unfamiliar dress, unless they can themselves be endowed with a past, and in varying degrees a consciousness of it. I cite, and will presently consider, an example of this variable consciousness. Gray, enchanted with Cumberland, tells Wharton of paths over the fells between Derwentwater and the coast in a region 'barr'd to prying Mortals'; 'for some weeks in the year it is passable to the Dale's-men but the Mountains know well, that these innocent people will not reveal the mysteries of their ancient kingdom, the reign of Chaos & old Night.'[1] He is expressing, only half in play, the general belief that mountain-dwellers are secret people with a peculiar knowledge of the past. The relevance of this belief to Scott and Stevenson, though obvious, has not been sufficiently considered.

In attempting to understand the sense of the past we shall encounter three factors to be reckoned with: notions, part figment, part vision, as they existed in the mind of the

---

[1] *Correspondence of Thomas Gray*, ed. Paget Toynbee and Leonard Whibley (1935), III. 1088.

story-teller; these as they grew in the receptive minds of the original readers, and as they have remained constant through the centuries and are discernible in our habitual thought. To isolate any of these would be an idle exercise, but, since it is necessary to begin somewhere, I shall try to characterize that sense of the past which works in those of us who have lived some while and, for much of it, have read and observed; who have, moreover, carried their reading back into former ages. In such minds, the past may be likened to a terrain lying beyond a watershed: on this side stretches the familiar and intelligible landscape of the present. Not only can we see it; we have seen it by daylight and twilight, in summer and winter, and know what its salient features signify. On the further side, we must suppose, the streams run the other way; but, if it is the past of our own country, it cannot be wholly different from what we see and know—a counterpart with variations. For this interplay of likeness and difference we must sometimes rely on imagination. This may well seem a slender support, but the imagination is, as Johnson says, 'a licentious and vagrant faculty';[2] or, in more lenient terms, resilient and pliant. Like every other faculty, it should be employed but must sometimes be humoured. It will vouchsafe impressions of the past in distinct, brief insights. Its power to reveal former states of being is not sustained or continuous. I can liken it only to those clear but momentary glimpses of the opposite shore that you see among the Western Isles when the mist is drawn like curtains across the intervening water.

This suited Scott, whose method was episodic. Or perhaps it would be fairer to say that it tempered for him the convention of the three-volume novel to which he usually subjected himself. As an example of the strength and weakness of this method, a passage from *Guy Mannering* will serve: it stretches from the morning of Harry Bertram's fifth birthday to nightfall on that same day, when his death is accepted as certain.[3] Throughout those hours—or that chapter—the tension is relentlessly sustained; but when Godfrey Bertram has turned

---

[2] *Rambler*, no. 125.
[3] I. 131–50; Chapter ix.

back to his desolate home with the cry '"Wife and bairn, baith—mother and son, baith—Sair, sair to abide"', it is broken, never to be renewed: 'a space of nearly seventeen years' intervenes. Meanwhile the law has taken its ineffectual course, and when we return to Ellangowan with Mannering that tragic day has become a subject of fireside gossip in the Kippletringan inn—predictably humorous.[4]

Once only Scott achieved perfectly sustained tension throughout the three episodes, of unequal length but equal significance, which spanned a tale: 'The Two Drovers'. But the full-length novel, to which Ballantyne forced him back, was beyond the scope of such continuous vision: during its course, insight would come and go. (Even the carefully planned political and military framework of *Henry Esmond* would not hold but for the sense of a personal destiny awaiting the hero.) There is however an alternative to the unitary structure of the novel. The device of successive short stories, separated by intervals of oblivion as dreams are sometimes separated by intervals of sleep, makes *Puck of Pook's Hill* and *Rewards and Fairies* a singularly happy invention. At the end of 1827 Scott told Ballantyne that he wanted to 'lie fallow'—not (as I read the plea) to give up writing, but to stop publishing 'for a year or two'.[5] What the *Chronicles of the Canongate* might have been if Ballantyne and Cadell had not harried him,[6] we shall never know.

The flash of insight suited Scott's mind: he had a well stored memory abounding in illustrative anecdote, and, although he could very well survey an historical situation when occasion required it, he preferred illustration. It suited his social habits also: a visit to a familiar place in congenial company would evoke incident, with a pregnant phrase of dialogue to point a tale and give it an air of spontaneous recall.[7] But the extension of this hospitable relationship from guest to contemporary readers must be credited not only to his genial temperament but also to good fortune: the time of

---

[4] I. 173–89; Chapter xi.
[5] *Letters*, Grierson, X. 329; 17 Dec. 1827.
[6] Grierson, *Sir Walter Scott*, p. 274.
[7] Mary Anne Hughes, *Letters and Recollections of Sir Walter Scott*, Chapters ii and viii.

writing (from *Waverley* to *Redgauntlet*) was propitious in that he and they stood at the right distance from his subjects in the Scottish novels. Culloden was his watershed, and theirs—as Bosworth had been Shakespeare's. (Has anyone reckoned the number of novelists for whom it was Waterloo?) The Forty-Five had left a deeper impression than the Fifteen: a whole generation had been obliged to come to terms with the idea of a 'foreign' army on 'native' soil. The aftermath was but too well known. How much would still be remembered of the executions on Tower Hill? There had surely been nothing like them since. As for the subjugation—or pacification—of the Highlands which followed, the quick succession of books and pamphlets on the state of that region throughout the next half-century shows that here were disquieting matters to be faced and a widespread anxiety to understand them. Scott might count on just so much knowledge as would prompt a willingness to be better informed. The novelists had not hitherto been very lavish with information; they had been too busy preaching, teasing, or cajoling. Maria Edgeworth's *Castle Rackrent*, to which Scott paid generous acknowledgement, was an exception, but it was, and remained, singular: she herself never wrote anything quite like it, and its next-of-kin seems to me to be *The Real Charlotte*—which again stands by itself, in the Somerville and Ross canon.

Waverley was well timed for an opening move in this new game. That does not mean that Scott had no more to do than reach out and grasp opportunity. Though he had not to create, he must still cultivate the taste by which he was to be enjoyed. We can hardly suppose that every reader even then, and even in Scotland, would start at the mention of 5 May 1679.[8] When Scott, who is sparing of dates, set that in the forefront of *Old Mortality*, he clearly expected a knowledgeable response, and by 1816 he may have been able to count on it. If so, it was the measure of his achievement. Today's reader probably owes such acquaintance with Scottish history as he can claim to Scott, and to the later novelists who built on his foundation.

---

[8] Two days after the murder of Archbishop Sharp.

When Stevenson writes of Scott's 'hopeless merit' and couples this with his 'defects',[9] I think he means merit which is the despair of emulation, no matter what the shortcomings. Scott will always be the challenger, the initiator. There had never been anything quite like *Waverley* in the history of that ingratiating, bright-eyed mongrel, the novel. If it had not been completed and published—and by Scott's own account it came near extinction at an early stage—we might perhaps never have known the historical novel, which has strengthened that mongrel's capacity for survival. The history play would make fitful reappearances, quickly acclaimed and soon forgotten; the verse romance set in the past would persist to the end of the Victorian age; the tawdry 'period piece' might have come into being—but not the real thing. We should then miss a vision of the past established and thriving in a region where the imagination carries on its serious business, independent of the vagaries of fashion. Others have been free to develop, and sometimes to improve; but Scott's magnitude—which is not quite the same thing as greatness—forbids them to originate: his scope is so wide that nearly all the possibilities of historical fiction are latent in his work.

Waverley is the right starting-point for considering Scott's sense of the past, and not for reasons of chronological propriety alone. He will pursue the Jacobite tale further and, in *Redgauntlet*, achieve an incomparably finer ending; he will explore the historical situation more fully and more subtly in *The Heart of Midlothian*; but *Waverley* in simple terms announces his theme: the persistence, in the Highlands and the Isles, of an almost unimaginably remote and ancient order of society. This is linked with the movement which brings it to light, the Jacobite cause, by illustrative episodes.

The theme is given out in 'A Postcript, which should have been a Preface'—that is, the last chapter of *Waverley*: 'There is no European nation which, within the course of half a century, or little more, has undergone so complete a change as this kingdom of Scotland.' He enumerates the forces which have 'united to render the present people of Scotland a class

---

[9] *Letters*, Colvin, III. 306; to Colvin [from Vailima], 'November 16th or 17th', 1891.

of beings as different from their grandfathers, as the existing English are from those of Queen Elizabeth's time'.

The progress of the rebellion is not Scott's concern. What he offers to the reader who will follow the hero's erratic course from Waverley Honour to Edinburgh is a succession of insights which hindsight may interpret as contributory causes. The archaic constitution of Highland society is the most important but not the sole factor in the historical situation. In other parts of Scotland, and here and there in England, we are shown men and women who feel themselves to be living *between two wars*. To live thus is to be the prisoner of events, caught between memory of the past and expectation of the future. This is the state of things which Scott conveys through his depiction of three households. I do not include that of Donald Bean Lean, if household it can be called, because it illustrates only a timeless lawlessness, very different from the conditioned and nicely measured dissent of those three.

At Waverley Honour there are intimations that English Jacobitism has burnt itself out. Sir Everard Waverley had taken no part in the rising of 1715, though he had used his wealth on behalf of Jacobite prisoners after it was put down. Even this activity, with his avowed sympathies, will have repercussions upon the story, but on no heroic scale. For his sister Rachel the lost cause has become an old and plaintive song; an elegy for past sacrifices and a childless future.[10] Behind these two lurks the younger brother, Richard Waverley, performing on the tight-rope of political opportunism. And, still of this older generation, the non-juring clergyman, Mr Pembroke, testifies by his presence to the political complexion of the household, and also to its enervating climate. Edward Waverley himself, with his desultory education and romantic inclination, is a product of the past, though his ingenuous countenance bears little mark of it, whereas the ambiguity of his situation is clearly signalized in the circumstances of his entry into active life. By a nice turn of irony, his aunt's anxiety to remove the idle, susceptible boy from the first woman he fancies himself in love with miscarries:

[10] I. 46–9; Chapter iv.

foreign travel is ruled out by 'the unhappy turn of Sir Everard's politics'.[11] So Edward must seek worldly experience in the army; and Sir Everard's valediction is clouded by a conviction that it is the wrong army. (By a further turn of irony, Edward will not remain in it for very long.) Sir Everard's speech is a little masterpiece. Even a brief extract will show its quality:

'My dear Edward, it is God's will, and also the will of your father, whom, under God, it is your duty to obey, that you should leave us to take up the profession of arms, in which so many of your ancestors have been distinguished.'

He assures his nephew that he has made suitable arrangements for sending with him not only horses but also men from the estate.

'. . . and, sir, in the field of battle you will remember what name you bear. And Edward, my dear boy, remember also that you are the last of the race, and the only hope of its revival depends upon you; therefore, as far as duty and honour will permit, avoid danger—I mean unnecessary danger —and keep no company with rakes, gamblers, and whigs, of whom it is to be feared, there are but too many in the service into which you are going. Your colonel, as I am informed, is an excellent man—for a presbyterian; but you will remember your duty to God, the church of England, and the . . . [the King sticks in his throat and he contents himself with] all constituted authorities.'[12]

All this has been appropriate preparation for the portrayal of a different sort of Jacobitism in the Baron of Bradwardine's household at Tully-Veolan. There, when the Baron welcomes Edward as the nephew of the man who befriended him after the '15, we meet another clergyman without cure. He is a symbolic figure, unemployed in the story. Scott marks his significance in a brief passage, lit by a single line from Dryden's 'Character of a Good Parson':

The non-juring clergyman was a pensive and interesting old man, with much the air of a sufferer for conscience sake. He was one of those,

[11] I. 59; Chapter v.
[12] I. 75-6; Chapter vi.

Who, undeprived, their benefice forsook.

For this whim, when the Baron was out of hearing, the Baillie used sometimes gently to rally Mr. Rubrick, upbraiding him with the nicety of his scruples. Indeed, it must be owned, that he himself, though at heart a keen partizan of the exiled family, had kept pretty fair with all the different turns of state in his time; so that Davie Gellatley once described him as a particular good man, who had a very quiet and peaceful conscience, that *never did him any harm.*[13]

The Baron's own situation is more complex, and must be inferred from a brief retrospect and a number of allusions. His politics have forbidden practice at the Bar and sent him into foreign service—making of him one of Scott's favourite types, the soldier-pedant. His intervention in the '15 has isolated him, compelling him to live in solitary, feudal state, and foster his other pedantry, genealogy.[14] It will gradually become apparent that he, a scholar and a soldier with a distinguished record in the foreign wars, is confined to the society of his inferiors. Flora Mac-Ivor, brought up at the French court and holding (for political reasons) archaic Highland state at Glennaquoich, stigmatizes the company Edward has met at Tully-Veolan as an unhappy product of 'the ruthless proscription of party'.[15]

There is no need for the novelist to expatiate on the likeness and difference between Sir Everard's self-imposed isolation and the Baron's virtual imprisonment on his own estate—where he will eventually be more closely confined in his cave of refuge. Likewise, the non-juring clergymen at Waverley Honour and Tully-Veolan are nicely differentiated. At the close, Mr Pembroke will complain that, so long as Sir Everard was in danger, his own meals were always half-cold.[16]

Presently, Edward Waverley is transported—rather by Scott's design of illustration than by the logic of the story— to the Mac-Ivor stronghold, and discovers yet another sort of imprisonment, partly self-imposed. His host presents himself, before his own gate, attended by 'about an hundred Highlanders, in complete dress and arms'—although the household's scanty stores of forage are guarded from the half-wild cattle and ponies by a few boys and a famished dog. Fergus apologizes negligently for this display, but puts his troops through their military exercises. His talk, however, presently betrays the fact that he is the prisoner of his own grandeur: the Highlands having been ostensibly disarmed since the '15, he may not appear outside his own territory with his private army, while the state he chooses to keep will not allow him to appear without it. The last imprisonment will be in Carlisle gaol.

A problem confronting the historical novelist, to which I must from time to time recur, is the two-fold necessity of involving his fictitious characters with the persons and events of history at the outset, and extricating them at the close. For Scott in particular this means releasing his heroes from the tragic issue of those events. Edward Waverley is rescued from the consequences of his Jacobite adventure and all its implications by romantic contrivances, and by the pattern of a good turn repaid which was dear to Scott's heart. Moreover, he is released from obligation to his former cause by the tacit forgiveness of the Mac-Ivors. (True, they had drawn him in, Flora by deliberate exertion of her charm, Fergus by subterfuge.) More to the purpose, however, is the question, how he comes to forgive himself so easily. But Scott is resourceful: Edward's horror at the ruin of those two lives—apparently, his sole response to final defeat of the cause in which he had joined them—is softened into melancholy by his endeavours to communicate it to Rose Bradwardine: in a series of letters he comes to see their terrible end as he wishes her to see it.[17] And so he enters into the comfortable heritage of the English eighteenth century. Apart from the maimed beggar at Mrs Flockhart's door, and a chilling reference to 'one or two' of the Baron's servants who 'had not been heard of since the affair of Culloden',[18] remembrancce of that day is obliterated, as Colonel Talbot, in Scott's favourite part of fairy godfather, restores Tully-Veolan to its former state.

The Jacobite tale, part history, part myth, is not the only source of that sense which Scott can convey of the past as

[17] III. 331; Chapter lxx.
[18] III. 217; Chapter lxiii and III. 360; Chapter lxxi.

agent—something which still works in human affairs through present consciousness. I have tried to describe the impress of a former event in terms of terrain: a watershed. Now, reverting to that quotation from Gray's letter to Wharton with which this chapter began, I ask indulgence for my landscape metaphor. In a deeply fissured region, the inhabitants of neighbouring valleys may have little intercourse, but they are aware of one another's presence, and will probably cherish a traditional sense of their diversity. Tradition plays a part in the Lowlander's idea of the Highlander; and tradition maintains that the Highlander is anchored in the past. Throughout 120 years, from Johnson's *Journey* to Stevenson's last fragmentary writings, this was the refrain. The Highland Line may be drawn by geology and its human consequences from Stonehaven, through Dunkeld, Comrie, and Aberfoyle, to Helensburgh. But it seems as though, for Johnson, Scott, or Stevenson, the Highlands begin just where he comes to feel this undertow of the past. Johnson, it is true, thought he had missed the very thing he came to seek.[19] Nevertheless he listened to tales of that vanished dispensation. Scott, coming into the world later but to the task much younger, was able to save from oblivion that past which older men remembered. Stevenson, apart from what he could learn in Appin, had to rely on written sources—but then, those sources included Scott. Yet, so closely was that other way of life, once led alongside one like ours, associated in Scotland not so much with a triumphantly secret people as with the idea of a perpetually losing side that, whereas the fall of the Stuarts affords its context in most of the stories embodying it, the sense of a tragic destiny can attach itself to other lost causes. Indeed, I doubt whether any Stuart departure is more than a symbol. After all, like other famous theatrical families, they were noted for 'positively last appearances'.

An unsympathetic observer of the situation in the mid-eighteenth century alleges that devotion to the Stuarts was always contingent on their absence: 'The MacDonalds pretend that their Attachment to the Stuart Family proceeds from a Principle of Loyalty and Duty but it is observable of several

[19] *Journey to the Western Islands of Scotland* (1775), 144–5; Yale Johnson, IX. 64–5.

Highland Clans . . . that they have been mostly loyal to some King or other who was not in Possession, and when they could not find a Pretender they never were at a loss for a pretence of some kind or other for Rapine and Plunder.'[20]

Whatever the motives for their loyalty—or intransigence—they paid dearly for it; and their plight lent to their neighbourhood an air at once archaic, tragic, and menacing. This is implied in that account of their condition which Bailie Nicol Jarvie gives to Frank Osbaldiston: it ranges from their poverty at home to their precarious livelihood as migrant reapers, haymakers, and shearers, who 'may make some little thing for themselves honestly in the Lowlands.'[21] That summary was enough for his day; but for Scott it was not enough. In the very heart of *Marmion* a strangely anachronistic, strangely moving passage had betrayed his own awareness of a later and sadder chapter in the story: the evictions. Breaking impetuously into that pasteboard romance, he tells us that the air of Constance's song was such as he had heard the harvest bands sing:

> Oft have I listen'd, and stood still,
> As it came soften'd up the hill,
> And deem'd it the lament of men
> Who languish'd for their native glen . . .

Regardless of the context, his mind moves forward to another and irrevocable exile: how would it sound beyond the Atlantic,

> When heart-sick exiles, in the strain,
> Recall'd fair Scotland's hills again![22]

These images of exile are not without dignity. Familiar as we are with their appearance in poetry, we may fail to recognize another less stately: the Highlander as a poor urban immigrant. It was well known to Scott. At the time of the

---

[20] *The Highlands of Scotland in 1750*, from Manuscript 104 in the King's Library, British Museum, ed. Andrew Lang (Edinburgh, 1898), pp. 53-4.

[21] *Rob Roy*, II. 280; Chapter xxvi.

[22] *Marmion*, Canto III, stanza ix.

Porteous riot, 'the soldiers of the City Guard, being . . . in general discharged veterans . . . and being . . . for the greater part Highlanders, were neither by birth, education, or former habits' well fitted to handle unruly bystanders, and were soured by the indignities they had often suffered.[23] In Scott's own boyhood, the old Highlanders of the Town-guard were helpless, with their Lochaber axes, against youthful turbulence.[24] Janet MacEvoy, herself a reassuring link between past and present for the returned wanderer Chrystal Croftangry, has a piteous tale to tell of the Highland immigrants in Edinburgh, outcasts from the dispeopled glens.[25] All these figures, whether ludicrous or pitiable or both, have an air of belonging to the past, recalling not only 'battles long ago', but all 'old, unhappy, far-off things', to which their presence in a later and very different world bears witness.

It is Stevenson who finds words for this sensation of living alongside survivors from an earlier world: he invokes the 'Celtic race, deprived for so many centuries of their authentic speech, surviving with their ancestral inheritance of melancholy perversity and patient, unfortunate courage.'[26]

All this allows the novelist who takes Scottish history for his province to gather within it characters for whom the distance between past and present is not the same, thereby giving fulness and depth to his vision. But he has still to communicate this heterogeneity in his 'field full of folk.' There is moreover that other problem, of giving coherence to a long story fitfully illuminated by flashes of insight. Scott found a solution for both in the tradition of the English novel. Stevenson was to use it once; then strain it, and at last venture beyond it.

The tradition which Scott inherited tends towards successive rather than consecutive episodes, linked by the part played in all of them by the hero. His freedom of movement gives diversity to the scene—mobility is usually the chief, sometimes the only, asset of these young gentlemen. To their travels in space Scott and Stevenson are able to add travel in

---

[23] *Heart of Midlothian*, I. 71; Chapter iii.
[24] Lockhart, *Life*, I. 81.
[25] *I Canongate*, pp. 89–95; Chapter v.
[26] *Heathercat*, Edinburgh edition, Vol. XXVI; Chapter i.

time. But this raises yet another problem, to which even Scott finds only a partial solution. Is the 'hero' as he conceives him a proper instrument for his purpose? In *Waverley* and (with variations) in *Rob Roy* and *Redgauntlet*, the hero is swept into a past of which he had formerly no cognizance. Fortune, the presiding genius of romance, determines his movements; and romance, a tolerant spirit, asking little of the players in its game, can be trusted to give a sense of urgency to that journey. We accept it as a flight from evil or quest for good, of which the outcome matters very much to the traveller, and we want to know whether he arrives. For Edward Waverley, Frank Osbaldiston, and Darsie Latimer as romantic heroes, this is enough. But how can such incurious minds communicate to us a sense of the strange worlds they have passed through? In *Waverley*, Scott maintains a distinct authorial presence. With dry detachment he conducts his hero past menace of which he is unaware, and notes signs he cannot read. It is he, and not their commanding officer, who tells us that the inferior Highland troops, victims of an archaic system, were wretchedly armed.[27] If Waverley's discovery that he does not understand the language of the men he is supposed to command is merely the first step in his extrication from a false position, we may read in it Scott's epitaph on the Jacobite cause.[28]

Scott forfeits this ability to communicate directly with us when he resorts to first-person narrative in *Rob Roy* and letters in *Redgauntlet*. There is room, in the wide conventions of the novel, for the narrator who tells us more than he knows; but this requires a vein of irony alien to Scott's genius. In default of such irony, dialogue which is clearly beyond the comprehension of the hearer who reports it must draw heavily on make-believe. Though it is necessary, and therefore allowable, that, in a story told by one of its characters, long passages of talk should be recalled, this serviceable convention is surely strained when Frank Osbaldiston, one of Scott's most obtuse Englishmen, reproduces faultlessly those significant idiomatic differences in the exchange between Rob Roy and Nicol Jarvie. Yet this idiom is the key to that

[27] II. 328–9; Chapter xliv.
[28] II. 351–2; Chapter xlvi.

former world which Scott intends us to enter. Darsie Latimer's incomprehension of his own and his country's past is essential to the plot; but it is left behind, together with the convention of letter or journal—which has already worn paper-thin—when Scott becomes sensible of the need to unfold those larger issues in which the true interest of *Redgauntlet* consists. Such issues he can throw into sharp relief, whether he takes up the tale himself or frames illustrative passages of dialogue. Nothing more vividly conveys the difference between Highland and Lowland assumptions than the exchange between Rob Roy and Nicol Jarvie when they meet in the Glasgow Tolbooth[29]—nothing, that is, until David and Alan are brought face to face in Appin.

Story-telling of this sort is, in some degree, an art of discovery. Conscious choice and design are not the only factors to be reckoned with. We all hope to build a little better than we know; without such hope, who would ever begin? But where hope is solicited there will be corresponding fears. The story-teller is likely to cherish an almost superstitious veneration for the forces at work in that region of his imagination from which his stories come. Kipling, in *Something of Myself*, has much to say about his 'daemon'. Scott, afraid lest he should fail under pressure, talks to his *Journal* of dependence on his 'magic wand'.[30] Stevenson, recalling Scott's years of forced labour, utters the fear of 'that hour when the pastime and the livelihood go together.'[31] Superstition is implicit in his acknowledgement of indebtedness to dreams—he would sometimes refuse to discard an implausible detail because the dream had furnished it.[32] Moreover, having inherited or learnt from his father the trick of putting himself to sleep with stories of his own invention, he would indulge in fanciful impersonation and be 'much engaged in Jacobite conspiracies' as sleep overtook him.[33]

[29] II. 202-8; Chapter xviii.
[30] *Journal*, p. 65 (22 Jan. 1826).
[31] *Letters*, Colvin, III. 159; to James Payn from S. S. Lübeck, 4 Feb. 1890.
[32] *A Chapter on Dreams*, Edinburgh edition, Vol. I, and *Life*, II. 14. In *The Strange Story of Dr Jekyll and Mr Hyde*, 'The powder was condemned as too material an agency, but this he could not eliminate, because in the dream it had made so strong an impression upon him.'
[33] ibid.

It is not easy to define the difference between this dreaming, partly willed and partly the involuntary sequel to make-believe, and his access to deeper sources in *Kidnapped*; but it can be perceived and illustrated. He speaks with justifiable pride of David and Alan walking out of the canvas,[34] for the book lives by virtue of their life; they live by virtue of their relationship; and that relationship sprang from knowledge as well as imagination. It was not there at the outset, like his dream situations; he discovered it in the very act of setting them in their historical context. Into an essay[35] which he contributed to *Scribner's Magazine* in 1888, but which (understandably) he did not include in any collection nor propose for inclusion in the Edinburgh edition, he inserted a supposed confession by a 'writer of fiction whom I have the advantage of knowing'—a subterfuge he sometimes used to fend off the charge that he wrote too much about himself.

'In one of my books', he writes, 'and in one only, the characters took the bit in their teeth;[36] all at once, they became detached from the flat paper, they turned their backs on me and walked off bodily; and from that time my task was stenographic—it was they who spoke, it was they who wrote the remainder of the story. When this miracle of genesis occurred, I was thrilled with joyous surprise; I felt a certain awe—shall I call it superstitious?'[37]

Graham Balfour, quoting from this passage, tacitly identifies it as a reference to *Kidnapped*.[38] How did this 'miracle' come about?

Stevenson had made David Balfour the narrator—perhaps for no better reason than that he had fallen into the way of it with Jim Hawkins and this was to be another boyish adventure story. David, unlike Frank Osbaldiston and Darsie Latimer, is by no means vacuous. He lacks, however, the lively curiosity and keen appetite for experience of Kim.

---

[34] *Letters*, Colvin, II. 296; to Watts-Dunton from Skerryvore, [Sept. 1886.]
[35] *Some Gentlemen in Fiction*, reprinted in Vailima edition, XII. 311ff.
[36] Vailima, 'in their mouth'—which is nonsense.
[37] op. cit., XII. 311-12.
[38] *Life*, II. 16.

After all, he never wanted to see the Highlands. His aim, constant though persistently thwarted, is to return whence he came—I do not say, to return home, for Edinburgh is not his Ithaca; it is merely the place where he purposes to establish his claim on the revenues of Shaws. Yet, despite his intention and against his will, experience penetrates and transforms his view of life.

Superficially, the story takes the first turning towards its destination in an incident which recalls *Treasure Island*: David, like Jim Hawkins, overhears plans for treachery, and warns the intended victim. But, whereas in the former tale the boy was of the threatened party and had every reason for his action, here he takes the part of a stranger, a Jacobite— which he has been brought up to regard as at best a strange animal—and throws in his lot with one whose chances of survival seem negligible. 'I have no credit by it; it was by no choice of mine, but as if by compulsion, that I walked right up to the table and put my hand on his shoulder. "Do ye want to be killed?" said I.'[39] And that is how such a friendship should begin.

Thereafter, David is learning to survey, and communicate to us, the landscape of the past which stretches back from the Highland Line. At one level, that of observation, he discovers a primitive world, of dire poverty, but still with traces of an archaic order. Cluny keeps a chieftain's state in his 'cage': 'I had a fair chance to see some of the inner workings of a Highland clan; and this with a proscribed, fugitive chief; his country occupied; the troops riding upon all sides in quest of him, sometimes within a mile of where he lay; and when the least of the ragged fellows whom he rated and threatened, could have made a fortune by betraying him.'[40]

Language now becomes a symbol of alienation. David has no gaelic. On the one hand there are those Highlanders who will speak English only at a price; on the other, those who courteously insist, at some cost to themselves, that only English shall be spoken in his presence. He finds himself a stranger in what he had assumed to be his own country, speaking a language which his supposed countrymen regard as foreign.[41]

---

[39] Chapter ix.   [40] Chapter xxiii.
[41] See pp. 148-153 below.

It is at a much deeper level of understanding that he reluctantly follows Alan into a world he had never envisaged. And, when something beyond mere observation is to be conveyed, the novelist who speaks through one of his characters has a balance to strike between insight and hindsight: between what the narrator apprehended as he underwent an experience, and how he comprehended it afterwards. David has entered the story as a mere boy; one who has never left his native parish of Essendean. He has to communicate to us matters which would naturally lie at the furthest reach of his own understanding, if not beyond it. True, he undergoes suffering which might well force growth; and it is likewise true that, if the development should still seem too rapid, we shall be content to accept minor anomalies in return for the major satisfaction of losing ourselves in the story; we shall not complain if David suffers as a boy and speaks as a man.

Ripening begins when, in the heat of their common peril and shared escape, David learns from Alan to see the affair of the tenants on the Forfeited Estates as something more than political fact. He catches sight, also, of the tribal warfare, more bitter even than antagonism to the ruling power, which rends the Highlands.[42] To a fellow Lowlander, Mr Henderland, he will owe a brief vision of those absolute loyalties—' "no perhaps Christian, but humanly fine" '[43]— into which he will himself be drawn by his friendship with Alan. It is in the wood above Lettermore that he crosses an invisible Highland Line into a primeval world. And this, surely, is where these two characters walk out of the canvas. A man of moderation, considerations, reservations, becomes sworn brother to one who lives by absolute values—and those the very reverse of his own. To Alan it is self-evident that the guilty must be protected at whatever cost, because they are more vulnerable than the innocent.

'They that havenae dipped their hands in any little difficulty, should be very mindful of the case of them that have. And that is the good Christianity' . . . When it came to that, I gave Alan up. But he looked so innocent all the while, and was in such clear good faith in what he said, and so ready

[42] Chapter xii.
[43] Chapter xvi.

to sacrifice himself for what he deemed his duty, that my mouth was closed. Mr. Henderland's words came back to me . . . Alan's morals were all tail-first; but he was ready to give his life for them, such as they were.[44]

That innocence is in itself no safeguard Alan admits and David will come to recognize, when he is called to bear witness for James of the Glens: James hangs and David himself narrowly escapes suffering with him. The completion of *Catriona*, however, lies seven weary years ahead, with *The Master of Ballantrae* intervening. How much of *Catriona* Stevenson had in mind when exhaustion compelled him to abandon David at the door of the British Linen Company's bank and reserve his further course for a possible sequel,[45] we cannot know for certain; but it is a fair surmise that he saw his way clear to the trial at Inverary, and perhaps not far beyond that natural culmination. The rest, as he acknowledged, is really another story,[46] in which Alan's fidelity, now in some sort shared by David, will be contrasted with James More's—Macgregor allegiance being notoriously transferable.

Thus the hero of a novel drawn from Scottish history can travel through a past which is for its other characters their present, his powers of perception and communication depending on his author's cunning. Yet, supposing this position accepted, the reader who happens to be English will here object: the past may be perpetuated in terms of thought and feeling, but how are the senses—notably the eye—engaged? Where are the visible traces of human habitation by former generations? There are none. To the eye of poetic sensibility, mountains may speak of ancient mystery; but they are mysterious because they turn a blank face to this very question. The Highlands, unlike the English landscape, are not man's handiwork.

> See you our little mill that clacks,
> So busy by the brook?
> She has ground her corn and paid her tax
> Ever since Domesday Book.

* * *

[44] Chapter xviii.
[45] *Letters*, Colvin, II. 283–4; to his father [from Skerryvore, Apr. 1886].   [46] ibid., IV. 19; to Colvin from Vailima, 2 Mar. 1892.

Trackway and Camp and City lost,
Salt Marsh where now is corn,
Old Wars, old Peace, old Arts that cease,
And so was England born![47]

Sussex may be exceptional, and Kipling's Sussex the quintessence of that exception; but, throughout the length and breadth of England, an undisturbed village is a piece of history. And, where greed has not devoured it, English landscape speaks to the eye in the shape of field or copse, the direction of hedgerow or lane, to the ear in their names, of a past reaching further back than history. But that very handsome cultivation of the Lowlands has scarcely lasted three centuries, and a traveller who trusted the dictionary's definition of a clachan would look for a village in vain.

This may go some way towards explaining why there is scenery rather than landscape in Scott's novels: scenery in front of which his characters act out their parts. Out of doors, within doors, still something is wanting—the impress of long habitation and the sense that people and places are alike inheritors of the every-day happenings of many generations. Want—absence—can these be illustrated? Perhaps not; but it is possible to mark the point at which expectation is disappointed. Monkbarns, the home of Jonathan Oldbuck in *The Antiquary*, promises well. It has its place on the map—near a seaport on the east coast of Scotland.[48] More to the present purpose, it is situated in time: like its owner—and all Scott's substantial characters—it has its pedigree; it was the bailiff's house, and is now all that remains of a former monastery. It presents an image to the mind's eye: random additions make it appear, like many Scottish country houses, as though it had been built room by room. The heart of it is Oldbuck's own room. This is where (so far as the storyteller is concerned) life is carried on. But it has nothing to say of the generations of Oldbucks who have called Monkbarns their home. It is merely a receptacle for the accumulated purchases of the present owner, the hoard of a human magpie. Scott was ready to laugh at his own antiquarian dabblings; even to admit credulity. Oldbuck's ill-assorted collection

[47] *Puck of Pook's Hill*: 'Puck's Song'.
[48] Supposedly Arbroath.

prepares us for his discomfiture at the Kaim of Kinprunes. ('"From this very Praetorium"—A voice from behind interrupted his ecstatic description—"Praetorian here, Praetorian there, I mind the biggin o't." '[49]) But had there not already been a more naked self-exposure than Scott himself intended? Monkbarns is disconcertingly like Abbotsford—which had no history. The objects which were bought to fill it could not even simulate a family home. It is true that antiquarian studies fell far short of our present scruples and solicitudes; but Scott's practice seems to have been, even by the standards of his day, primitive if not barbaric. He tells unabashed how, coming away from the cave in which the islanders of Egg had been massacred by the Macleods, he 'brought off, in spite of the prejudices of the sailors, a skull, which seems that of a young woman'.[50] The sailors very properly blamed him for the adverse winds they encountered.

Now, it is true that Scott is not simply Jonathan Oldbuck: in so far as this is a portrait and not a Theophrastan character, it is composite.[51] Nevertheless he did associate himself with 'the Antiquary'—and this not merely retrospectively in the 'Reliquiae Trotcosienses'.[52] Oldbuck assures Lovel: 'The very least boy that can herd a cow, calls it the Kaim of Kinprunes, and if that does not imply an ancient camp, I am ignorant what does." '[53] That sounds like an echo of a memorable phrase in the *Minstrelsy*: 'The least child that can herd a cow will tell the passenger, that there lie "two lords who were slain in single combat." '[54]

It is pleasant to set over against Scott's 'gabions' an imaginary, and imaginative, collection which Stevenson salvaged from his vagrant life. This is the inventory of Billy Bones's possessions which Jim and his mother find when they ransack

[49] I. 77; Chapter iv.

[50] Lockhart, *Life*, II. 430. See also Robert Stevenson's account, in *Reminiscences of Sir Walter Scott, Baronet*, published by his grandson in *Scribner's Magazine* (Oct. 1893).

[51] Scott is believed to have drawn on characteristics of George Constable, John Ramsay of Ochertyre, and others. See W. S. Crockett, *The Scott Originals* (1912), pp. 123-9.

[52] The catalogue of Abbotsford curios which Scott was compiling when he died. See Grierson, *Sir Walter Scott*, p. 293.

[53] I. 71; Chapter iv.

[54] Introduction to 'The Dowie Dens of Yarrow'.

his seaman's chest for money to pay his debt to the Admiral Benbow; and Stevenson recalls how it came into being. He had been reading the early chapters of *Treasure Island* aloud to his family—notably, his 12 year-old stepson.

I had counted on one boy; I found I had two in my audience. My father caught fire at once with all the romance and childishness of his original nature. His own stories, that every night of his life he put himself to sleep with, dealt perpetually with ships, roadside inns, robbers, old sailors . . . . In *Treasure Island* he recognized something kindred to his own imagination . . . and he not only heard with delight the daily chapter, but set himself actively to collaborate. When the time came for Billy Bones's chest to be ransacked, he must have passed the better part of a day preparing, on the back of a legal envelope, an inventory of its contents, which I exactly followed . . . [55]

That is in the sturdy tradition of Defoe, but with an added bounty: it reaches back into a remembered past, and we know and trust the man in whose memory it has been preserved. He knew all about the old sailor's Spanish watch, quadrant, pistols, and the rest—and the 'five or six curious West Indian shells'.[56] He knew they would be there; he did not know why; and that is what makes the tally convincing. A comparable anecdote is recounted in *Something of Myself*:[57] Kipling's father, a lover of craftsmen's skills, took over from his son the description of Harry Dawe's penknife, in 'Hal o' the Dract'.

Things, as the novelist and essayist must know, are evocative; and none have more of this inherent power than artifacts—objects made, handled, used by man. But, as a means of bringing back the past, they are not always tractable. Lord David Cecil contemplates *Vanity Fair* from this point of view:

The effects of time . . . are the occasion of some of Thackeray's most characteristic triumphs. He had a special sensibility to

---

[55] 'My First Book', Edinburgh edition, Vol. IV.
[56] *Treasure Island*, Chapter iv. Only the chart is required by the story.
[57] p. 188.

the relics of the past; what more poignant emblems are there of man's transitoriness and vanity? Old pictures, old toys, old letters with their yellowing paper and browning ink . . . . George Osborne's room opened after years to show a half-finished scrawl on the writing-table . . . these things never fail to touch him to a sort of poetry; the faded, ironical, plaintive poetry, so sad and yet so mellow, of memory.[58]

But it must be the historical novelist's aim to show some of these things in their first freshness. The ruined castles inhabited by the characters of 'Gothic' novels are a standing joke. Wear and tear are permissible, but not dilapidation—unless some special circumstance in the story calls for it. The Green Room, at Monkbarns, with its old-fashioned tapestries, serves a purpose: it is the setting for Lovel's mood of disquietude, and—more pertinently—the occasion for Oldbuck's reflections on the insulting permanence of things.[59] (We all enjoy being sententious about Time.)

Under a wider survey, it will appear that, at the very deepest level of tradition, lies one kind of thing: the token. It is buoyantly used in romance.

> O got ye it by sea or got ye it by land?
> Or got ye it off a dead man's hand?

You may not recognize your husband, come home from sea, but you are never mistaken about his ring.

Shakespearian romantic comedy had made such simple devices respectable, and Scott uses them lavishly in the interest of the happy ending. Harry Bertram is identified as the rightful heir by the contents of a little velvet bag which his mother hung round his neck when he was 5, and which is still there some seventeen years later, and after much hardship and many perils. Why should a novelist discard any contrivance that his readers are willing to accept?

As the novel advances, however, in cunning workmanship and a claim to be taken seriously, its authors come to realize that they are playing a game of which they themselves have made up the rules—may even be making them up as they go along. The conventions of an easy-going dramatic tradition

---

[58] *Early Victorian Novelists* (1966), pp. 77-8.
[59] I. 211; Chapter x.

will no longer serve. (They never had, even for the stage, once Shakespeare's magic was lost.) How is time to be treated—above all, distant time? In *Esmond* the problem is comparatively simple: an old man remembers, for the benefit of his grandchildren, past events in which he was once involved. Thackeray is careful about Queen Anne's London; and the convention of first-person narrative allows the narrator to oscillate between memory and re-living. We cannot fairly demand even and consistent filling in of all visual detail. Some particulars will naturally be taken for granted.

Kipling was in a unique position; and we shall best understand what he is about if we begin by likening him to a man playing with models, of his own devising: *things that work*. Many forces joined in him. From his father he had his veneration for craftsmen and craftsmanship; from his circumstances, as a returned exile, his passionate desire for evidence of continuity. These, together with something in himself, made him resolve not only to *read* things but also to make them tell their story. He would meet difficulty with intricacy; he liked both, for their own sake.

In the treatment of time, Kipling set himself a peculiar problem by going outside the natural order of things. What he is writing, in *Puck of Pook's Hill* and *Rewards and Fairies*, might be called fantasy; but it is so radically serious that I would rather call it myth. (It is much more serious than the ostensibly veracious story of the American exiles who discover, by signs and tokens, that they *belong* in Sussex.[60]) Granted this power to bring back the past as a momentary present, Kipling sets himself to fulfil Puck's promise to the children' ' "You shall see What you shall see and you shall hear What you shall hear, though It shall have happened three thousand year." '[61] Men and women come back from the past, even the very distant past, and relive their lives as they talk to the children. Sometimes there is a variation in the pattern: Dan overhears Hal of the Draft's second tale, as it is told to his present-day counterpart, the old builder.[62]

---

[60] 'An Habitation Enforced', in *Actions and Reactions* (1909).
[61] *Puck of Pook's Hill*: 'Weland's Sword'.
[62] *Rewards and Fairies*: 'The Wrong Thing.'

Twice Puck tells the tale himself.[63] Once he impersonates a dead friend of Hobden, that bastion of tradition, and tells it as that friend might have recalled his wife telling it.[64] One characteristic prevails throughout: boldness—this is no dateless world of mere fantasy. When Sir Richard Dalyngridge acknowledges that he has disguised names and armorial bearings of the people in his story for fear of offending their 'children's children', Puck applauds: ' "It is knightly to keep faith—even after a thousand years." '[65] When Puck teases Simon Cheyneys, he remonstrates: ' "Oh, Mus' Robin! 'Tidn't fair. You've the 'vantage of us all in your upbringingin's by hundreds o' years. 'Stands to nature you know all the tales against every one." '[66] Even more boldly, Sir Richard comforts Una when she grieves for his sorrow: ' "Little maid, it all passed long ago." '[67] He is reliving his former life, with a clear consciousness of distance. How can the gossamer web of illusion bear this strain?

It holds because it is intricately woven; and in this very intricacy we may find the answer to that simple-seeming question: are we drawn to the people of the past by their likeness, or unlikeness, to ourselves? The difference must be enough to stimulate imagination; not enough to baffle it. Or, to look at it the other way round: there must be likeness sufficient for fellowship, but not so much that we feel these to be the characters of any romance, trimmed up to please idle fancy. They must offer fresh insight.

Kipling chooses supernatural means: these forerunners return. He had practice, and cunning, in the representation of haunting—such visitations as assail the overtaxed mind and body. *But these are spirits of another sort.* Their credentials are (for the most part) such things as may testify to the continuity and fruitfulness of ordinary life: the farm, the mill, the forge, and what was made there. A single exception points this generalization: though 'Dymchurch Flit' is strong in its sense of place, it has few tokens of habitation and

---

[63] 'Weland's Sword,' and *Rewards and Fairies*: 'Cold Iron.'
[64] *Puck of Pook's Hill*: 'Dymchurch Flit'.
[65] *Puck of Pook's Hill*: 'Old Men at Pevensey'.
[66] *Rewards and Fairies*: 'Simple Simon'.
[67] 'Old Men at Pevensey'.

handiwork—because the distress which is its theme remains intangible; likewise, the relief. Elsewhere, the *thing* may witness to a sombre past, but it has been absorbed into common use and serves the purposes of daily life. Told of the means by which a stricken village would ensure supplies in time of plague, Dan asks: ' "Where did we put the plague-stone? I'd like to have seen it." "Then look at it now", said Puck, and pointed to the chickens' drinking-trough . . . It was a rough, oblong stone pan, rather like a kitchen sink, which Phillips, who never wastes anything, had found in a ditch and used for his precious hens.'[68]

In *Something of Myself*, Kipling volunteers to explain how it all began. Settled in Sussex, and indefatigably improving his English estate, he found, wherever spade or mattock penetrated, pieces of history stretching back even through Roman Britain to the neolithic age. 'Every foot of that little corner was alive with ghosts and shadows.'[69] Place and things conspired. With family encouragement and help, most notably his father's, he found this tale not merely legible, but communicable. After discarding some false starts—he did not practise Scott's frugality—he found himself carried buoyantly through successive divinations—intuition verified. But there is, surely, one kink in the line. 'I had put a well into the wall of Pevensey Castle *circa* A.D. 1100, because I needed it there. Archaeologically, it did not exist till this very year (1935) when excavators brought such a well to light. But that I maintain was a reasonable gamble. Self-contained castles must have self-contained water-supplies.'[70] Yet in both the tales which turn on the existence of this very well it is—and has to be—tidal, and brackish. ' "I made it for a drinking-well" ', says De Aquila; but it proved useless—so it was not the castle's water-supply.[71] Exultation had played a trick on memory.

Of his own aims and methods he says that the tales were designed to be read variously by various people. This is not

---

[68] *Rewards and Fairies*: 'A Doctor of Medicine'.
[69] p. 186.
[70] ibid., p. 189.
[71] *Puck of Pook's Hill*: 'Old Men at Pevensey'; also, 'The Treasure and the Law'.

the happiest kind of complexity: it leads to interventions by Puck, with the time-dishonoured injunction: 'not before the children'. 'I worked the material in three or four overlaid tints and textures, which might or might not reveal themselves according to the shifting light of sex, youth, and experience.'[72]

Those of us who are affronted by Kipling's habit of whispering behind the hand[73] may choose rather to contemplate another and more innocent sort of guile which is at his command. He has a many-sided problem to solve when the children encounter the story-tellers. How are the senses, the mind's eye and mind's ear, of the reader to be fed? It is through what the children hear and see that we receive our impressions of these strangers; but, if anything were to seem strange to *them*, the spell defending them from 'doubt and fear' would be broken. How then can anything in the appearance of these figures be signalized as remarkable? Can difference of dress, for example, be noted—and the children's implicit acceptance of all they see remain undisturbed? With one notable exception, Kipling avoids such details of dress as Charles Reade assembles. Harry Dawe's 'plum-coloured doublet and tight plum-coloured hose', with hair which 'bristled out in a stormy fringe'.[74] agrees unobtrusively with early Tudor portraits, and so will serve for a first impression. But some first impressions may need to be sustained by quiet, incidental reminders. When Sir Richard stirred, his old horse, 'hearing the chink of his chain-mail, looked up and whinnied softly'.[75] It comes home to us as something which has happened before, and will again, so long as chain-mail is worn.

The exceptionally detailed description of dress in 'Marklake witches'[76] has a purpose to serve. Philadelphia Bucksteed describes her newly worn finery to Una—neither girl knowing that Philadelphia's to-day is, even by mortal standards, transitory. Stevenson's devising, with Isobel Strong's help, of pretty clothes for young Kirstie Elliott[77] had a different aim.

[72] *Something of Myself*, p. 190.
[73] . . . ' "he burying his best friend, Mus' Doughty"—"Never mind for Mus' Doughty" Puck interrupted': 'Simple Simon'.
[74] *Puck of Pook's Hill*: 'Hal o' the Draft'.
[75] *Puck of Pook's Hill*: 'Young Men at the Manor'.
[76] *Rewards and Fairies*.   [77] *Memories of Vailima*, pp. 70-1.

Given this conjunction of time, place, and the things which make place into environment, the Sussex stories are bound to stand apart. Kipling's imagination works powerfully on the Wall; memory and regret sharpen his sense of what Philadelphia must have been like in the days of its primitive piety; but in Sussex he has only to feel with his hands in the brake to find those evocative things. This does not mean that the Sussex stories are always the best. Besides knowledge there must be love. 'Gloriana'[78]— a failure, in my estimation—shows what happens when it is absent: the speaker is an unwilling visitor to Rye, an impatient sharer in its public, superficial life. The impression is cold and metallic. There is the same coldness in 'The Treasure and the Law'. Life and sap flow through tales in which Sir Richard raises his arms 'as though he would hug the whole dear valley',[79] or Hal whispers ' "D'ye wonder that I love it?" '[30] Here place, time and things are all in a tale together.

So it appears that, whereas Scott and Stevenson, with their eyes upon

> a little patch of ground
> That hath in it no profit but the name,

speak to the mind in general terms, such as can be formulated, Kipling, with his heavy freight of ideas, speaks to the senses by evoking particulars, a diversity of little, familiar things. Can the difference between English and Scottish history account for this paradox? G. M. Young seems to suggest as much: 'The lack of historic memory has been noticed as an English characteristic. But generations of firm government had left us with nothing to remember'[81]—at least until taste veered towards a new sort of historical writing and vision, a concern with the tenor of life betweenwhiles. Critical assiduity can usually offer a choice of explanations, but they seldom explain everything.

[78] *Rewards and Fairies.*
[79] 'Young Men at the Manor.'
[80] 'Hal o' the Draft.'
[81] 'Scott and the Historians', *Sir Walter Scott Lectures*, pp. 90-1.

Chapter III
Historical Insight
and the Story-Teller

It will, I believe, prove expedient to distinguish between a
sense of the past and a sense of history. In all argument,
some agreed distinctions are necessary. In literary criticism,
a game played according to few and variable rules, no more
than convenience can be claimed for many of the distinctions proposed, but I hope that this one may earn acceptance
by its usefulness.

According to Philip Mason, Kipling possessed a sense of
the past, but not of history:

> In the sense that he could put himself in the position of
> Queen Elizabeth or a Roman centurion, he was a magnifi-
> cent historian, but he was no historian at all in the sense of
> perceiving the currents of thought in history.[1]

His reference to Kipling's misreading of the imperial theme,
notably in terms of South African politics, suggests that we
must understand him to mean currents of political thought
in their bearing on political experience, past, present, and
future.

Is this failure of political sense to be inferred simply from a
misinterpretation of those lines which converge—or seem
from our standpoint to converge—out of the past on to the
present, and a misjudgement of their promise, or threat, for
the future? Hindsight makes censure easy, but not all Kipling's misgivings, nor those of Scott, now seem so ill founded
as they formerly did. In fairness to both it may come to be
said only that neither was very willing to think again. This is
hardly surprising, since the two enjoyed, each in his day,
supreme popularity in the realm of imaginative literature.

---

[1] Philip Mason, *Kipling: The Glass, The Shadow, and The Fire*
(1975), p. 197.

To frame an estimate of the speed and direction of political currents which will satisfy future generations, better furnished as these must be with knowledge of the sequel, requires uncommon sagacity; and sagacity is not a property of the imagination, though a few—a very few—imaginative writers have possessed it. Want of sagacity is not to be summarily equated with failure in the exercise of bringing imagination to bear on historical events and characters. There is still a further distinction to be proposed.

Two different motives impel us to look for those connecting lines between past and present, and perhaps to speculate on their future direction. One I have already considered as a factor in our preoccupation with the past: the desire for continuity.[2] This, as an emotional current, can be felt even when the writer is declaring that the line is broken, the very phase of past history he has lovingly evoked is

gone, gone, gone with lost Atlantis.[3]

The other is rational, relying on the expectation that, of two similar instances of human behaviour in given circumstances, the later may well be the outcome of the earlier. Within his own favourite field of reference—the idiom of thought and feeling in the individual man or woman—Scott is impregnable. He is handling less tractable material when the issue lies between factions and ideas. We cannot fairly demand infallible judgement of the novelist who takes such a conflict for his subject, nor a quite impartial estimate of the rights and wrongs to be weighed. In medieval art, St. Michael is often shown with sword in one hand and in the other a pair of scales, weighing the soul as it departs this life. In the one scale crouches the supplicating soul; in the other, or clinging to the underside of it, is a devil. It is surely enough if the imaginative writer so chooses and frames his subject that he can set human forms in either scale, even if this means that neither will appear wholly innocent.

Though civil war is the most tragic of all conflicts, yet it allows the belief that something might be said on either side. There can be no two thoughts about an invading army;

[2] See introduction and p. 14, above.
[3] *Rewards and Fairies*: 'Philadelphia'.

about King and Parliament there may be—afterwards; seldom at the time. To judge fairly and write temperately about the '45 was not, to a man of Scott's time and temper, very difficult—at least, so long as he said little of the immediate sequel. On the one side, sense—a sense of the possible; on the other, suffering. He was free to pity and even admire the losers, without wishing they had won. The conflict between Covenanters and government, singled out (even in Scottish history) as 'the Killing Time' was more stubborn material.

The writer of fiction, free to present things as they might have been, and probably anxious to extricate his hero from the calamity of things as they were, is likely to make him a moderate, a just man torn between conflicting claims. This is Scott's favourite way, and Henry Morton his typical hero. Let him be embroiled for honour's sake—the memory of his father, the cause of Scottish independence; he can be rescued from the extremists of his own faction in payment of a debt owed him by his adversaries, and released from obligation to his chosen cause by the parole he has given to his rescuers. Time will do the rest. Foreign service and return after the Revolution will furnish all that is needed for the happy ending—and bring him nearer to our (doubtless fair-minded) selves.

The moderate man, whom events conspire to preserve, is a serviceable if not very sympathetic hero. Scott found a more reassuring scheme for *Redgauntlet*: he shifted the time-interval. The lapse of twenty years between armed conflict and the opening of the story has allowed Darsie to grow up in the belief that the issue of the '45 is past history. He has never been involved in the Jacobite cause, and his uncle's tragic involvement merely offsets, with its darker colour, his freedom to enter a peaceful present. Thackeray, whom I believe to have been influenced by *Redgauntlet*,[4] likewise aligns the propitious time-interval with the passage of the generations: Henry Esmond, a political agnostic rather than a moderate, has no difficulty in leaving behind him the issues which the Revolution has determined.

[4] See pp. 117–119, below.

The pains of choice will await his grandsons, but in another cause.

The obligation to choose between conflicting claims is not, however, the sole issue in a tale of civil war. The question, how the campaign was conducted on either side, may trouble us more deeply. This Scott knew well, and *Old Mortality* illustrates his knowledge, and his insight into the behaviour not only of individuals but also of groups under the pressure of their common aim or ambition. Contrast dominates its structure, but there are underlying resemblances. In tragic opposition, Ephraim Mcbriar's intransigence is set against Lauderdale's cruelty, the arrogance of Balfour of Burley against that of Claverhouse. In a romantic dance of fortuitous rivalry and mutual generosity, Morton is paired with Evandale. The spirit of comedy locks Mause Headrigg and that most reluctant of martyrs, Cuddie, in conflict with Lady Margaret Bellenden. Scott was blamed in his own day for bias against the Covenanters. He had held the balance fairly in historical writing: 'The Covenanters deny to their governors that toleration, which was iniquitously refused to themselves.'[5] In fiction he is not on oath: a little play may be allowed to his distrust of theocracy—particularly when it assumes military command. But there is one element in his treatment of the Royalists which his critics seem to have overlooked. It is not so much what contestants assert—the rights they claim, the methods they defend—that shakes confidence. It is what they appear to take for granted. The language of the Royalist leaders (unlike that of their opponents) is not uniformly outrageous. It ranges from Claverhouse's occasional outbursts of intolerance to Miles Bellenden's regretful acceptance of the conditions of civil war. But they one and all acquiesce in the maintenance of their own ascendancy by means of the dragoons. If a man is to be known by the company he keeps, he may well fear a more humiliating exposure in the character of the agents he employs. The dragoons are tools forged for the purposes of oppression—of which the oppressor need not know too much.

At length, treading delicately, Scott sets the New Testament

---

[5] *Minstrelsy* (1803), III. 210.

faith and practice of Bessie Maclure over against the course
which the Covenanters suppose to be enjoined on them by
the Old Testament. But I find an even more explicit judgement in a letter which he wrote on 6 September 1828. John
Richardson had congratulated him on making amends to the
Covenanters in the Second Series of *Tales of a Grandfather*,
to which he replied:

As to Covenanters and Malignants they were both a set of
cruel and bloody bigots and had notwithstanding those virtues
with which bigotry is sometimes allied. Their characters were
of a kind much more picturesque than beautiful cast [sic].
Neither had the least idea of toleration or humanity so that
it happens that so far as they can be distinguished from each
other one is tempted to hate most the party which chances
to be uppermost for the time.[6]

This passage penetrates into the response, not only of the
novelist but of every shrinking, appalled reader of history,
where such a conflict is the subject.

Happily, not all history lies under the shadow of politics.
Social history, though akin to political, has its own dial and
its own sun. It can tell the time in the light of family chronicles,
showing how inherited temperament and tradition react to
political fluctuations which it is the business of other historians to spell out. Was Scott the first to discover that family
history need not be veracious? I know of no earlier novelist
who invents pedigrees to serve his purpose. Sometimes it is
a bold, sufficient sketch: the Oldbucks, descendants of
German craftsmen, once refugees from religious oppression,
have upheld the Protestant succession in Fairport, but have
never been completely assimilated by the townspeople—far
less by the gentry of the neighbouring countryside. Sometimes it is a finished masterpiece, as when the Bertram family
history is used to set the scene for *Guy Mannering*.

This is a story of the decline, almost to extinction, and
the hair's breadth rescue, of the ancient house of Ellangowan.
Behind Godfrey Bertram, as Scott presents him, stretches
the record of a family which, remaining still in one district,

[6] *Letters*, Grierson, XI. 59.

isolated and stagnant, has reacted to the course of political history, generation after generation, by invariably backing the losers, until worldly decline has reduced even this response to inertia. Nothing is left but a touchy pride which some turn of circumstance may inflame to transient and ineffectual activity. Bringing the young Mannering to Ellangowan, Scott makes us understand the significance of what he sees, by means of a recapitulation of this family history, symbolized by juxtaposition of the old castle and new house. With Mannering, we enter Ellangowan Place and recognize in Godfrey Bertram the product of declining fortunes and surviving pretensions. There is dramatic irony in his petulant expostulation: 'You'll be surprised to hear it, Mr Mannering —but I am not a justice of peace.'[7] Likewise his treatment of Meg Merrilees, designed to impress Mannering with his standing among the gypsies,[8] will presently be recalled with fuller understanding of its ominous overtones.

Mannering departs. The child whose horoscope he has cast grows into an active little boy, and wheels begin to turn. A fresh political change seems likely, for the first time in its history, to benefit Ellangowan, and Godfrey Bertram attains his fancifully cherished ambition. His commission as Justice of the Peace is read aloud to him, 'and at the first words, "The King has been pleased to appoint"—"Pleased!" exclaimed he, in a transport of gratitude; "Honest gentleman! I am sure he cannot be better pleased than I am." '[9] It is the beginning of his downfall. In his elation, he flourishes the new broom. The gypsies and smugglers are the inevitable victims of his self-assertion. But he has been too familiarly associated with them to allow a painless severance; and so his path plunges forward and down, to violence on either part and eventual disaster.

Fielding, perhaps even Smollett, might have given us someone like Godfrey Bertram, something like his downfall; but only the thoroughbred historical novelist can represent the precipitation of a crisis as the culmination of a process.—And all this, where the persons and events are, in the time-honoured phrase, unknown to history.

[7] I. 76; Chapter v.   [8] I. 38; Chapter iii.
[9] I. 92-2; Chapter vi.

Scott showed the way for others to follow, but I doubt whether any of them has yet caught up with him. Thackeray, as Geoffrey Tillotson points out,[10] liked to build up interlocking patterns of family history; but, in the one novel where they might have served that very purpose for which Scott employed them—one, moreover, in which Scott's influence is evident—they fail to fulfil their function. The dominant theme in *Henry Esmond* is Stuart ingratitude. Hindsight in the writer of a memoir allows it to run like a refrain throughout. By the end, it is seen to have determined the course of the story, and even resolved Esmond's inner conflict. It has been persistently stigmatized as ingratitude to the whole Castlewood family: loyalty and sacrifices have been repaid, at best with trumpery honours, at worst with dishonour. The effect may resemble the tragic farce of Amelia's devotion to George Osborne; but, whereas that can be accepted as the outcome of her character and situation, this amounts to a family hallucination. Loyalty may indeed be misplaced; but, where it is shared and continued through characters so diverse and so variously situated as the Esmonds and Castlewoods, it requires a motive. It is not, of course, necessary that the particular Stuart prince whom the novelist has chosen to illustrate his theme should deserve the devotion he throws away, but we must be given some warrant for believing in his power to attract it. History might allow the Old Pretender to be ineffectual; Thackeray imposed profligacy on him, for his plot's sake; but could he afford to make him downright insignificant?

Scott's Prince in *Redgauntlet* may be only the ghost of his former self, but his past has been heroic and, like the setting sun, he throws long shadows. His father, in *Esmond*, throws no shadow at all. Before he comes to England he is commended as being more presentable than the future George I—which would not be difficult. When, on arrival, he turns out to be not only worthless but negligible—and Thackeray will not even trouble to see him out of the country—we are obliged to ask what credence and what credit we can give to loyalty satisfied with so poor an object. Among the women

[10] *Thackeray the Novelist* (1954), pp. 5-8.

of the Castlewood family, the dowager Isabel and Beatrix Esmond may be the stuff of which kings' mistresses are made; and that, for the cynic in Thackeray, is sufficient attachment. But the most constant and disinterested loyalists —until the exposure—are Rachel Castlewood, Henry Esmond who (after the decline of Father Holt's influence) sets his course by her, and Frank Castlewood, who sets his by Esmond. Rachel, however, with the shadowy presence of the Dean her father behind her, comes out of another world than that of the old court, its Jacobite intrigues and ambitions. And so a further element of ambiguity is introduced into this elusive character. Seen in retrospect, the Jacobite or loyalist tradition in Castlewood family history appears a mere spectacle, a dance—led and (for the most part) performed by the women; therefore, since Thackeray is the choreographer, a symbol of fantasy. It engages the eye but fails to satisfy the mind, and so contributes nothing to the historical authenticity of *Esmond*.

Family history is not to be looked for in *Kidnapped*, where an orphan joins forces with an outlaw; and, if David Balfour's forgetfulness of anything in his past earlier than his arrival at the House of Shaws amounts to amnesia, we must remember that the story was planned 'partly as a lark, partly as a pot-boiler'[11]—and came to life when David met Alan.

I have so far considered the story-teller's historical insight chiefly in terms of penetration: the fairness with which he enters into a critical situation, and his use of family history as a means of entry. This, however, is only a part of his problem. No matter how he gets in, he must find his own way of integrating his people and events with the historical situation in which he has set them. Stevenson's first full-length historical novel affords a striking and curious example of this problem.

The *Master of Ballantrae* promises much. There is, if not a family history in the full sense of which the term is capable, a family situation; and, set in a period well documented and

---

[11] *Letters*, Colvin, II. 296; to Watts-Dunton from Skerryvore, [Sept. 1886].

still remembered, it brings to a head the tensions in that situation by means of the impact of an historic event. That is the classic opening: Henry Morton falls in with an assassin of Archbishop Sharp; Reuben Butler is caught up with the lynching of Porteous. Moreover, Stevenson uses a circumstance which was well attested in the history of the successive Jacobite risings, and of which he had a particular instance in mind: when the Stuart standard is raised, a family decides to send one son to either contestant for sovereignty, in order that, whatever the outcome, the estate may be secure. His warrant for this was written clearly in the Atholl family records.[12] Whether it was the best opening for his purpose is another matter. Could such deadly antagonism between brothers begin with the spinning of a coin to decide which of them should go 'out' and which should stay? The Master asserts that it did, but he is the least trustworthy of witnesses, especially in his final phase of self-pity.[13] It is strange that Stevenson should not bring Ephraim Mackellar, the witness on whom we are to rely throughout the story, to Durrisdeer until six months after the supposedly crucial day. True, that admirable narrator is able to reconstruct the occasion with vivid particularity—indeed, he does it so well that, if he had chosen to cast even further back, we should not ask how he came to know so much. But this is only the first, and perhaps the least, of many questions prompted by the handling of the story.

Stevenson himself had much to say of the origins and development of *The Master of Ballantrae*, but what he says bears less relation to its historical setting than do corresponding allusions to *Kidnapped* and *Catriona*. The principal passages are contained in two letters, written when he was newly engaged on the novel, and two retrospective accounts of its 'genesis', left unfinished, and published posthumously as fragments.

Of those two letters, the first, written to Colvin in 1887,[14]

---

[12] *Jacobite Correspondence of the Atholl Family* (Abbotsford Club, 1840). For Stevenson's concern with these letters, see pp. 70, 71, 75, 77, below.

[13] Chapter ix.

[14] *Letters*, Colvin, III. 35–6; from Lake Saranac, 24 Dec.

outlines the situation, enumerates characters, carries the plot as far as the duel, and dwells on the peculiarities of the Master. The second, to Henry James three months later, is more analytic and advances further into the story. I give the gist of this, and will revert to the other presently.

My novel is a tragedy; four parts out of six or seven are written, and gone to Burlingame. Five parts of it are sound, human tragedy; the last one or two, I regret to say, not so soundly designed; I almost hesitate to write them; they are very picturesque, but they are fantastic; they shame, perhaps degrade, the beginning. I wish I knew; but that was how the tale came to me however.[15]

He goes on to epitomize: that decision of 1745 to divide the family allegiance is given as the cause of disturbed and ultimately tragic relationships. He interjects: 'The devil and Saranac suggested the dénouement, and I joined the two ends in a day or two of constant feverish thought.' He is still unhappy about the result, but continues his epitome: the feigned death of the elder brother at Culloden, and his return to bleed the family; the duel, with his unlooked-for survival; and the 'steep' but picturesque catastrophe—all lead up to 'the death of the elder brother at the hands of the younger in a perfectly cold-blooded murder, of which I wish (and mean) the reader to approve'. The story is to cover eighteen years. Evidently he now has the whole course of it in his head.

Further light, but accompanied by baffling shadows, is thrown on this scheme by those later accounts of the way in which the novel developed. One of them may have been designed[16] as his contribution to the collected works—the Edinburgh edition which his friends had promised Stevenson. The note-book containing it was among papers of which Graham Balfour took charge for delivery to Colvin, and which he sorted out and transcribed. As 'The Genesis of "The

[15] *James and Stevenson*, pp. 170-1; [from Lake Saranac, Mar. 1888]. Both letters seem to envisage a shorter tale than the novel as we have it.
[16] Writing to Baxter from Vailima, 1 Jan. 1894, he speaks of a 'paper' he has drafted for *The Master of Ballantrae*: *Letters to Baxter*, p. 344. The context is a query about prefaces for the Edinburgh edition.

Master of Ballantrae"', it appeared in the Edinburgh edition
(Vol. IV), and thereafter in successive collected works. Of the
other, called a 'Note to "The Master of Ballantrae"', part was
first published in the Vailima edition, Vol. XXVI, and in the
Tusitala edition. Two further 'pages' (sc. leaves?) are in the
Huntington Library, and were transcribed and published by
E. N. Caldwell in her book, *Last Witness to Robert Louis
Stevenson* (1960).[17]

The 'Note' (as it appears in those two editions), after an
opening at once deprecating and defensive,[18] affirms Stevenson's interest in the story of the Marquis of Tullibardine,
eldest son of the first Duke of Atholl, who forfeited title and
estate to his younger brother on account of his Jacobite
sympathies and activities. After a lacuna, Stevenson resumes
what is clearly a claim that his Chevalier Burke is well enough
differentiated from Thackeray's Barry Lyndon. Then, still
whistling to keep his spirits up, in the essayist's manner, he
defends his employment of Mackellar as narrator; he weighs
the shortcomings of such a character against the 'realism of
method' which he attributes to first-person narrative.

The passage quoted in *Last Witness for Robert Louis
Stevenson*,[19] after a reference to this problem of method,
mentions, without naming them, persons who, falling within
his former range of observation, had served as models for
three of the principal characters—'I had been at school and
college with Mackellar and Henry'—and proceeds to this unaccountable assertion: for the Master, 'I had no original,
which is perhaps another way of confessing that the original
was no other than myself.'[20]

The 'Genesis' describes a night at Lake Saranac when three
several tales were in painful gestation: a rival to Marryat's
Phantom Ship; an account given to Stevenson by his uncle,
John Balfour, of an Indian practice—resuscitation by a fakir

[17] I owe my knowledge of the circumstances to the kindness of
Janet Adam Smith and her informant, Mr Ernest Mehew.
[18] Stevenson recommends that it be printed as an epilogue—the most
unassuming position. That is where it appears in the Tusitala edition.
[19] pp. 117-119.
[20] This, apart from its inherent improbability, is sharply at variance
with every other reference to this character, in these fragments and in
the two letters.

of one seemingly dead; and a Highland tale. The order of their emergence does not quite tally with the impression given in that letter to James. There, as in the scheme sent to Colvin, and by implication in the opening of the 'Note', the 'human tragedy' within a Highland family is the true source from which the novel springs. Here it seems more like an after-thought, drawn indeed from recesses of memory—but to supply a present need.

This is how Stevenson recalls the occasion: on that night at Saranac, his pleasure in *The Phantom Ship* prompts him to range through many countries and a stretch of time. Moreover, it leads him to reflect on the value of 'a familiar and legendary subject'—but that, he admits, came to nothing. Thence he passes to the anecdote of the fakir, and raises the question: what sort of man is to be resuscitated?—not in India, of which he knows nothing, but on the Canadian border. He decides on 'an evil genius'. 'And while I was groping for the fable and the characters required, behold I found them lying ready and nine years old in my memory.' That takes him back to a time when he was himself in the Highlands, and his mind was full of 'Athole correspondence', and another source of information.And here the devil really would seem to have intervened. Graham Balfour told what had happened, in a letter to *The Times Literary Supplement* (2 June 1921):[21] Stevenson's hand, in the last year or two of his life, could be quite illegible. 'Two words defied my utmost efforts, and I finally wrote them down as "dumlicide Justice". Apparently the editor [Colvin] could make nothing better of them, and as "Dumlicide Justice" they have engaged or escaped the languid attention of readers for a quarter of a century.' But readers can hardly be blamed when editor after editor repeated the blunder—among them Edmund Gosse, though he had been urged by Stevenson to read the book to which he is here referring.[22] More surprisingly, no one took any notice of the correction presently made by Graham Balfour in his *Life* (II. 31): by patient scrutiny, he discovered the true reading—'memoirs of the Chevalier de

---

[21] I owe this reference likewise to Janet Adam Smith and Mr Mehew.
[22] *Letters*, Colvin, II. 111; from Hyères, Apr. 1883..

Johnstone'. Even the correction made in the Vailima and Tusitala editions was not entirely helpful: 'memories of the Chevalier de Johnstone' does not point clearly to a printed book.[23]

Has this allusion of Stevenson's been thoroughly looked into? The relevance of the Atholl papers—correspondence among the Marquis of Tullibardine's Jacobite associates who insisted that he was still the true Duke of Atholl—is clearly relevant, so far as it goes. Here is a family situation which could well develop into family tragedy. The bearing of the Johnstone *Memoirs* on Stevenson's historical insight and imagination is not nearly so clear. One episode from them can be detached and considered on its merits; it is illuminating. This is that passage which Stevenson commended to Gosse in the spring of 1883. Johnstone urgently needed, in his flight after Culloden, to cross the Firth of Tay, from Forfar to Broughty Ferry; but the boatmen who should have rowed him over were frightened away by English dragoons. He therefore made himself so agreeable to the daughters of the inn-keeper with whom he had taken refuge that they rowed him across.[24] Sources are fragile things to handle: except in some very clear instances, I should hesitate to say 'B. would not have written this if he had not read A.'— never, 'he could not'. But, given that letter to Gosse in which Stevenson singles out the story of 'the dragoons, the timid boatmen, the brave lasses', it is surely evident that, having signalized it as worth telling, he presently told it himself, when he had to carry David and Alan across the Firth of Forth in the last and most hazardous episode of their flight. The interest, however, goes deeper than mere resemblance: as in all consideration of sources, it is the diversity of treatment that matters. If I speak of Stevenson's delicacy, I may seem to be praising a negative virtue—as though he merely refrained from giving offence; whereas it is here a positive quality. I can only ask the reader to observe Johnstone's insistence on

[23] Since Balfour returned the manuscript to Mrs Stevenson and did not see it again (see letter to *T.L.S.*, cited above), the balance of probability would be in favour of 'memories', but that Stevenson had written 'memoirs' in the letter to Gosse, cited above.

[24] *Memoirs of the Rebellion of 1745 and 1746* (1820), pp. 192-201.

the efficacy of his own flattery and kisses, here as in all his many encounters with women, and then to reread Chapter xxvi of *Kidnapped*. Alan's resourcefulness, his grasp of the situation, his lively consciousness of the three characters on whom his plan depends—David, the inn-keeper's daughter, and himself— all sparkle in the mind's eye: the play of light, the flicker of shadow, belong to a rare variant of tragi-comedy, in which cala- mity is averted, not by a flick of the author's wand, but by the native wit of a character designed for the purpose.

The relevance of the *Memoirs* as a whole to *The Master of Ballantrae* is less easily discerned; but Stevenson acknowl- edged it, and it cannot be ignored. I propose a separation into three parts: there is Johnstone's account of the rebellion, until Culloden; his narrative of his subsequent escape and service in the French army; and there are the Introduction and notes by the editor of the 1820 edition, whom I know only as J.B.—he is thus designated in the third edition. It is the first of these which has attracted the attention of his- torians, from that original editor to the present day, but which has no bearing on *The Master of Ballantrae*. The second could have stimulated Stevenson's imagination by its tale of hair's breadth escapes, though I have found no analogue half so clear as that crossing of the Firth of Forth in *Kidnapped*. The third has the most intrinsic interest, and (I reckon) the most measurable relevance. Johnstone himself smoulders with the dull resentment of the disappointed man. The spoiled only son of an Edinburgh merchant,[25] and a mere adventurer in the Jacobite cause, he maintains throughout the first half of the book that he could have conducted the campaign better than the commanders, on either side. In the second, his self-importance is swollen by self-pity. He regards everyone he meets as bound to further his escape—especially any woman. As a professed disciple of Rousseau, he expatiates on his own philandering. Scott inferred mendacity from one of the most ostentatious of these affairs, on the score that Johnstone was already married.[26] This inference is very

---

[25] Introduction (1820), p. xliii. See also Additional Notes to second edition, p. 5; and his account of himself, *passim*.
[26] Note to II. xxix of the 'Magnum' *Waverley*. I owe this and some other Scott references to Miss Claire Lamont.

much to Scott's credit, but hardly conclusive. Yet the linea-
ments of a liar are there. Stevenson attributes 'extraordinary
moral simplicity' to an acquaintance who served as model for
the Chevalier Burke;[27] Johnstone is a moral imbecile.

On this second part the editor scarcely comments, unless
to point out geographical and historical errors; but his interest
in the history of the rebellion is so keen that, in the first part,
the notes often swamp the text. He appears to be a well-
informed and informative historian, with a clear and consistent stand-point, and an incisive style. Though he was probably
working in London, he is plainly a Scot, and claims that he
was brought up among Presbyterians—whom Johnstone had
traduced.[28] He finds *Waverley* too romantic in its treatment
of the Pretender.[29] Where Johnstone, as adherent of Lord
George Murray, tended to criticize the Prince, he denounces
him, his claims, and the whole Stuart cause. Johnstone had
little to say in favour of the Highlanders; he was terrified of
them. J.B. judges them a dangerous anachronism. He undertakes to set the events of 1745 and 1746 in a context of
Scottish history, not of Jacobite myth. Herein I find the
most probable—perhaps the only tenable—explanation of the
appearance of three successive editions of this worthless
book.[30] Its tenor, as edited by a more practised writer than
the author, is dismissive, relegating Jacobitism to the past. It
must surely have been intended to serve a political purpose.

In assessing the importance of the *Memoirs* I put the editor
before the author. I cannot support this claim to his importance for Stevenson by any specific comparison; yet the
temper, the very voice, of J.B. is close to that of Mackellar—
or of David Balfour when, at Inverary, he discovers how
James Stewart's cause is regarded by his lawyers, for whom it
is a mere episode in tribal warfare. 'There was only one person that seemed to be forgotten, and that was James of the
Glens.'[31] Only David cares about the victim of this time-

[27] 'Genesis of "The Master of Ballantrae"', Edinburgh edition,
Vol. IV.
[28] Introduction, pp. xlvii-lx.
[29] See frequent references in the Introduction and notes; e.g. p.
xxxix, and note to p. 19.
[30] viz. 1820, 1821 (with Additional Notes), and 1822.
[31] *Catriona*, Chapter xvii.

honoured barbarism. And he cares because it is proper and becoming for the hero to experience a degree of sensibility beyond that of his contemporaries. But his judgement of the contestants, Campbell and Stuart alike, is that of his author, who is also his countryman, and J.B.'s. Although the epithet *Celtic* sounded emotional overtones in Stevenson's ear, he did not write sentimentally about Highland history.

The discrepancies within and among these accounts of the genesis of *The Master of Ballantrae* are numerous and some of them unaccountable; but it is what Stevenson does not say that teases the imagination. Though the novel is a frequent topic in letters to Baxter, and is mentioned elsewhere in his correspondence, any dissatisfaction with its development seems to be confined to the plausibility of the final catastrophe. No further doubts are raised after that letter to James as to its fitness to serve as culmination of the Durrisdeer tragedy. But the powerful concentration of tragic forces among the Duries can only be weakened by dissipation—the scattering of episodes in place and time, to which emulation of Marryat had incited Stevenson.[32] It is even stranger that he should be silent as to another departure from the theme which he had discerned in the Atholl papers. The Master does not merely caper about the world; he shifts his ground in another and more questionable way: still a pretended Jacobite fugitive, he becomes an active government agent. But the Marquis of Tullibardine had been a constant rebel from Sheriffmuir to Culloden, and died in the Tower. The plot may gain by this further entanglement, but history is slighted and the tragic tension broken.

All this suggests improvisation. A story-teller may improvise in either of two quite different states of mind: when the invention is full and overflowing, or when expedients devised to meet unforeseen difficulties themselves beget the need for further contrivance. A letter written when Stevenson was toiling to complete the story expresses discontent with the practice of publishing in numbers—the first committed to

---

[32] He tells Burlingame that the story 'jumps like a flea', but the context does not suggest dissatisfaction. *Letters*, Colvin, III. 39; from Lake Saranac in the winter of 1887-8.

print before the last is planned.[33] Structural problems may have proved more stubborn than he had foreseen.

This argument draws to a head with the assertion that *The Master of Ballantrae* is not merely a number of stories in one skin—something not unheard-of in the tradition of the English novel; it is composed of several incompatible kinds of story. A distinction must be allowed between incompatibility and incongruity. We have all watched incongruous couples making a success of marriage; but among those who are incompatible, none. Likewise in imaginative literature, the two states are distinguishable. Tragedy and comedy are manifestly incongruous; but, given genius to handle them, they are marriageable; and, because they *have* been handled by genius, we have come to accept their compatibility—perhaps too readily. Scott aims at combining tragedy with comedy in *The Bride of Lammermoor*; but that episode on shipboard, in *The Master of Ballantrae*, when Mackellar prays that the vessel may founder, and the captain, observing the fervour of his prayer but ignorant of the intention, thanks him for saving the ship,[34] has an edge of irony wanting in the tale of Caleb's blunders. It is besides more pointed and succinct.

The marriage of history with invented narrative poses its own problems. History will accept romance as partner, if the reader will but withdraw his critical faculties from the conclusion, as Scott requires. This is a comfortable convention, and, if we are inclined to demur at such a regard for our comfort, we shall not be reading this kind of book. Nevertheless, it shows a want of literary good manners in the writer if he treats a grave historical situation otherwise than seriously, before this separation of the partners, as it were by mutual agreement, frees him from any such obligation.

The historical situation in Scotland throughout much of the eighteenth century was indubitably tragic. Stevenson had chosen to set his story there, and then. His 'dead genuine human problem—human tragedy'[35] could have played itself out in the fathomless darkness of *Wuthering Heights*, where, despite mention of dates, there is no reference to public

---

[33] *Letters*, Colvin, III. 120; to W. H. Low from Honolulu, [20] May 1889.
[34] Chapter ix.   [35] Letter to Colvin, cited above.

events, and time is measured by the passage of the generations within a narrow circle of private life. He chose otherwise
—bewitched, it would seem, by the Atholl family history.
Committed to this, he was still free to follow out its implications, as Scott had done in *The Bride of Lammermoor*,
where faction lends weight to the family feud which destroys
the lovers. But on that night at Saranac, which appeared to
him so propitious, he took another course. He combined the
historical issue and the family tragedy with other, incompatible kinds of story.

A particular lie, well sustained and favoured by circumstance, is an accepted agent in fiction; and the Master's initial
lie bears this out. Moreover, we have learnt to our cost that
myth can outlive history. Therefore, when Alison and 'the
old lord', on learning that they have been deceived as to the
Master's death, modify rather than relinquish their postures
of mourning, we know that we are still within the bounds,
not only of narrative convention, but also (unhappily) of
common experience. But when the very spirit of falsehood
dominates the countryside, even in the Master's absence or
quiescence, as though by a sort of inherent superiority, then
we are surely moving into quite another region of story-
telling: moral fable, Hans Andersen at his most astringent.
Likewise the Master's own 'causeless duplicity'[36] is at variance
with the naturalism of the novel. Catherine Morland's solemn
discovery that 'a general though unequal mixture of good and
bad' is to be expected in human nature,[37] though it is pure
comedy, may convey Jane Austen's serious conviction that,
whatever the likelihood of 'unmixed' characters occurring in
life, they are not the proper stuff of the novelist's art.

How are we to understand a character to whom his author
attributes 'causeless duplicity'? The questions he provokes
reverberate. 'The Master is all I know of the devil.'[38] But is
he, in the last resort, the devil himself, or, as his final admission seems to imply,[39] that other legendary figure who has

[36] Letter to Colvin (III. 36), cited above.
[37] *Northanger Abbey*, Chapter xxv.
[38] Letter to Colvin; see note 36 above.
[39] Chapter x. He tells Mackellar: 'My life has been a series of un-
merited cast-backs.'

sold himself to the master liar and been cheated in the transaction?

It is a customary function of the central character in a novel, whether hero or villain, to hold the story together. but the Master, devil or devil's dupe, is not a unifying force. Hence the whole work is not greater than the sum of the parts. It may seem presumptuous to offer this opinion on a novel which Henry James called 'a pure crystal . . . a work of ineffable and exquisite art'.[40] But there is nothing to suggest that James ever thought of it as *historical* fiction, and his disregard for Scottish history had been betrayed in his characterization of Alan Breck as 'the little Jacobite adventurer'[41]—and that in a sympathetic review of *Kidnapped.* And, among the many and often brilliant components of *The Master of Ballantrae*, I believe the historical element to be the weakest. Even the scurrilous anti-Jacobite pamphlet which precipitates the final catastrophe looks like improvisation by a hard pressed but indefatigable contriver of plots.

I return to the question with which this chapter opened: what kind and degree of historical insight can we fairly ask of the story-teller who chooses to express his vision of human history in terms of fiction? We are not to look for the gigantic structure of historical theory informing Tolstoy's interludes and epilogues to *War and Peace.* These three authors are not philosophers. Fortunately they are poets; and, poetry being drawn from a deep level of consciousness, they may reveal in a poem, a stanza, even a line, something of the vision that haunted them. They had not to come to terms with such providential doctrine of history as was taught in England under the Tudors. Their vision was spontaneous and untaught. Scott's fundamental insight was not (so far as I can ascertain) derived from contemporary historians. It was his own, and it was tragic. His invocation to the Teviot contrasts the river, now flowing through a peaceful countryside, with another stream. It is

---

[40] *James and Stevenson*, p. 185; James to Stevenson, 21 Mar. 1890.

[41] 'Robert Louis Stevenson', written (and shown to Stevenson) in 1887, and published in *The Century Magazine*, and in *Partial Portraits*, 1888 (p. 147); also in the collection named in note 40 above, from which I derive these particulars.

Unlike the tide of human time,—
Which, though it change in ceaseless flow,
Retains each grief, retains each crime
Its earliest course was doom'd to know;
And, darker as it downward bears,
Is stain'd with past and present tears.[42]

This idea of cumulative misery far transcends mere exasperation, or even despair, at past errors. But Scott kept the sombre vision to himself, at least when he was writing the novels. Even in *The Bride of Lammermoor*, where political faction conspires with personal animosities to destroy the lovers, we are invited to draw no general conclusion as to our inescapable heritage.

To illustrate Kipling's vision I choose *'Cities and Thrones and Powers'*,[43] the flawless expression of his reading of a verse in the 90th Psalm: 'Thou turnest man to destruction: again thou sayest, Come again, ye children of men.'

Stevenson had little confidence in his own verse, and therefore entrusted to it less weight of reflection than to his graver prose. I look therefore to *Weir of Hermiston* for an answer to my question.

Weir of Hermiston promises unprecedented developments, and—left unfinished at the author's death—prompts as many unanswerable questions as *Sanditon*. Neither is elucidated by conjectures framed on a reading of previous works; each explores territory new to the writer. *Weir of Hermiston* registers the impression made on Stevenson by a well-known—indeed, notorious—historical figure: Robert Macqueen, Lord Braxfield. He had much to say about this origin himself. But, whereas Adam Weir is clearly to be regarded as a likeness, there is no such model for the family history in which he plays the principal part: that is a triumph of pure invention, quite unrelated to what is known of the Macqueens. It shows what Stevenson had learnt from his diligent work on the *Engineers*. This is not to say that he foisted any of his forebears into *Weir of Hermiston*.

The claim that Lord Hermiston is drawn both from Lord

---

[42] *The Lay of the Last Minstrel*, Canto IV, stanza ii.
[43] *Puck of Pook's Hill*.

Braxfield and from Thomas Stevenson—a very odd conjunction
—is based on certain correspondences. For the present, I
must be content to offset these with the (surely more notable)
differences. Robert Louis Stevenson suffered an estrange-
ment, of limited duration but of lasting effect, from his
father. Adam Weir and his son are, and always have been,
estranged; and only at one point is Archie's heart touched.
Moreover, since Thomas Stevenson had, in his son's estimation, too much religion, and Weir, like Braxfield, had, on any
reckoning, too little, the deepest source of anguish in the
Stevenson family finds no counterpart in either history or
fiction.

Another alleged use of Stevenson family history in the fictitious relationships of the novel links Archie Weir's parents
with Robert Louis's grandparents: both men, Robert Stevenson and Adam Weir, married pious wives, whose piety was a
hindrance to their housekeeping, and Robert's grandson
found plentiful illustration of this predicament in family
records and traditions. But, whereas Adam Weir is a domestic
tyrant, Robert Stevenson was tender to his wife and a merely
humorous martinet to the houseful of boys (his three sons
and their ten cousins) for whose upbringing he accepted
responsibility.[44] As for the two women, they share only the
narrow piety which made them employ incompetent servants
and tradesmen: Mrs Weir lived with her only child in solitary
imbecility, Mrs Stevenson in the midst of a numerous family,
and surrounded by 'godly parasites', as her grandson calls
them. Here then is a simple illustration of that powerful
alchemy which, though a natural process in the story-teller's
imagination, sometimes confounds the critical reason: a
family joke about Mrs Robert Stevenson's housekeeping is
transmuted into the tragic futility of Mrs Weir's life.

All this, however, is merely a part of that dense tissue
of family history which binds the characters and their destiny
in *Weir of Hermiston*. The distance which Stevenson had
to travel before work on his own family papers could
fertilize his imagination is illustrated by his early, fanciful

[44] *Manuscripts of R. L. Stevenson's Records of a Family of Engineers*,
Chapter iv.

speculations on his mother's ancestry. As an essayist, in *The Manse*,[45] he entertains conjectures of a Celtic origin for the Balfours, and plays with recollections of his maternal grandfather. There is some tentative curiosity as to our genetic heritage, lightly associated with references to the popular interpretation of Darwin's theory of evolution. He asks what 'tree-top instincts . . . gambolled and chattered in the brain of the old divine'.[46] In a later essay, he was to acknowledge such ideas as 'a new doctrine' too cursorily dismissed, 'and still not properly worked into the body of our thoughts'.[47]

Searching for Stevenson's deeper insight into family tradition and inheritance, we must begin with the 'daft-like marriage' of Archie's parents, and his descent on his mother's side.[48] Adam Weir comes out of nowhere. Like Heathcliff, he is apparently kinless in a world oppressively bound together by kinship—but there the resemblance ends, for he has established himself in his profession by signal abilities, has married an heiress and taken the name of her ancestral estate for his title. His hapless wife is the last of a line of freebooters who, marrying always submissive and downtrodden wives, have perpetuated their own fierce strain until, in their sole heiress, 'this succession of martyrs . . . took their vengeance . . . in the person of the last descendant . . . . She bore the name of the Rutherfords, but she was the daughter of their trembling wives.'[49] Whether or no this is genetically probable, the assurance with which it is related silences doubt.

There is, however, another strain of family heritage and tradition to be reckoned with. The history of the Elliotts has been as turbulent as that of the Rutherfords—with this difference, that all their contests were by force of arms: they did not use the law, they over-rode it. They belong to the Border, where trouble is always to be expected; and they are allied by blood with all the most contentious families in that ungovernable region. With an even bloodier history than the Rutherfords, they differ from them in being an unspent

---

[45] *Memories and Portraits*, 1887; it had appeared that year in *Scribner's Magazine*.
[46] Edinburgh edition, Vol. I.
[47] *Pulvis et Umbra*, Edinburgh edition, Vol. III.
[48] Chapter i.
[49] ibid.

force, plentifully supplied with children; the women, virtuous in respect of chastity, have been as stalwart as the men.

The link between Archie Weir and the Elliotts is not one of blood. It is of an intricacy and strength which could hardly be found outside that kinship-ridden society. Kirstie Elliott[50] claims eighteenth cousinship with his mother, through her own mother, who was her father's second wife. Thus she alone of the Elliotts has Rutherford blood. On the Elliott side, that of her half-brothers, she can trace a genealogy such as most families would be glad to forget, since 'from every ramification of that tree there dangled a halter'.[51] On the Rutherford side, and as housekeeper in poor Jean Rutherford's ancestral home, she had cherished a devotion to the ailing, failing mistress and a deep hatred of the tyrannical master, which he discovers only across his wife's death-bed.[52] It is characteristic alike of Lord Hermiston, of Kirstie, and of the constitution of an old-fashioned Scottish family that she should remain to rule Hermiston,[53] and that Archie's father should consign him to her care when he banishes him from Edinburgh.

When young Kirstie Elliott sings to Archie of 'their common ancestors', the tenderness and grief that move him join her image with that of his dead mother. 'So in all ways and on either side, Fate played his game artfully with this poor pair of children. The generations were prepared, the pangs were made ready, before the curtain rose on the dark drama.'[54]

This is the pitch of the singing rather than the speaking voice; but there is no change of key from the spoken narrative. The mention of Mrs Weir recalls Archie's childhood and the level tone of that family chronicle. In *Weir of Hermiston*, Stevenson achieves something which the scope and character of his former historical novels had forbidden: he communicates to us a sense of the tenor of life *betweenwhiles*—that is, when no crisis, historical or fictitious, is operative, or felt to be impending. Speaking of Robert Henry's division of his history into such topics as civil, military, religious, and so

[50] It will be convenient to call her Kirstie, and her niece young Kirstie.   [51] Chapter v.
[52] Chapter i.   [53] Chapter v.   [54] Chapter vi.

on, Johnson said: ' "I wish much to have one branch well done, and that is the history of manners, of common life" '[55] He would have waited a long while for it. This deficiency, until very lately, in historical writing can be illustrated, if not precisely measured. There are hardly any children. No doubt contemporary evidence was scanty: children, unless prodigies of learning or destined for an early death, went unrecorded. In *Kidnapped*, there had been no room for them nor for that 'common life' to which they bore witness. In *The Master of Ballantrae*, childhood is recalled only when Henry Durie is delirious,[56] and when his mind is finally giving way.[57] Family life at another level, but still following its normal course, might be expected when David Balfour makes part of Preston-grange's household. Its absence can be remarked by noticing how easily his exchanges with Barbara Grant could be transferred to the stage. As in artificial comedy, three panelled walls and a few eighteenth-century chairs would be enough. There is nothing behind that panelling.

Weir of Hermiston is built on a foundation of family life continuing through the generations; of common life in a particular time,[58] but set against a recollected past; and in a particular place, where former events have gathered to frame an intelligible present. There had been a notable scarcity of children in Scott's novels—apart from the vividly *recalled* childhood of Jeanie Deans and Reuben Butler. Among the Elliotts, they run about like young partridges on the ground. Archie is the product of his unnatural childhood: confined to his mother's company, dependent on her affection but developing a resistance to her illogical positions which begets a logical antagonism to his father. Here Stevenson succeeds in lifting, if only by a corner, the covering which had hitherto concealed the habitual life of his characters. (I say habitual rather than ordinary, for it is extraordinary to us.).

It is customary and convenient for the historical novel

---

[55] *Life*, Hill/Powell (1934), III, 333.
[56] Chapter vi.
[57] Chapter xi.
[58] For the question of Stevenson's purpose in shifting the date from the last decade of the eighteenth century to the second of the nineteenth, see p. 105, below.

to open with a crisis: some public event which, like a stone dropped into water, sends out widening ripples. But first there must be that still water—smooth, even despite uneasy premonitions. When the public event thus impinges on family life, we are sensible of that interplay of likeness and difference between our forebears and ourselves which whets the imagination. Family life is not the only symbol of continuity: Kipling found another to suit his purpose; that of guard duty —the centurion's service on the Wall,[59] de Aquila's self-appointed watch on the Sussex coast.[60] A sense of the tenor of common life need not immediately precede the crisis: in *The Heart of Midlothian*, Scott casts back to it.[61]

On 17 June 1894, Stevenson wrote at some length to his cousin, R. A. M. Stevenson, about their family tree, his own involvement in island politics, and the three books on which he was engaged. *St. Ives* is dismissed as a pot-boiler which he hopes to finish soon. 'After that I am on *Weir of Hermiston* and *Heathercat*, two Scotch stories, which will either be something different, or I shall have failed. The first is generally designed, and is a private story of two or three characters in a very grim vein. The second—alas! the thought—is an attempt at a real historical novel'—and he proceeds to characterize the 'killing time' in which it is set as one of peculiar interest.[62] Of *Heathercat* two chapters and part of a third were written; but this and other letters show that it would have been, in Kipling's phrase, 'ballasted on ingots of pure research'; and the fragment itself is heavy with Stevenson's early reading in the history of the Covenanters. In this sense it could claim to be the 'real historical novel', which *The Master of Ballantrae* had not been. Nevertheless, another and less obvious claim to that title might be advanced on behalf of *Weir of Hermiston*. Although in its five chapters—two of these incomplete—it pays little attention to public events, it commands resources of assimilated family history and the vision of a sombre inheritance.

[59] *Puck of Pook's Hill*: 'On the Wall'.
[60] *Puck of Pook's Hill*: 'Old Men at Pevensey'.
[61] See p. 92, below.
[62] *Letters*, Colvin, IV. 268; from Vailima.

Chapter IV

Historical Inspiration at Work, Notably in *The Heart of Midlothian* and *Weir of Hermiston*

These two novels seem to offer themselves for comparison—such a comparative view as may illustrate the workings of historical inspiration in a writer of fiction. Both touch the height of their authors' achievement; both disappoint, but for different reasons. In each, a spark is kindled by the writer's knowledge of a particular person, whose life (though not 'known to history' in the conventional sense) is on record, and the setting of whose career is familiar to him. No one but a Scot—perhaps none but a Scot reared in Edinburgh—could have evoked that setting. In each, this fire of inspiration burns with exceptional brilliance for a while, only to die and leave us in the dark. The cause of this extinction was, in Scott's case, chiefly expediency;[1] in Stevenson's, death. But in neither is this the whole story. There is a pattern to be traced, if not unravelled.

Of the manifold components of *The Heart of Midlothian*, three are indubitably historical: the Porteous affair, the tale of the woman who walked from Scotland to obtain in London a pardon for her sister, and the conduct of John, second Duke of Argyle, in relation to both. How Scott wove these together, and inserted into this dense historical fabric other strands, diverse in origin and character, is a story of which the outline is clear, though several details are obscure. If Stevenson was prone to tell too much, Scott, habitually secretive, told less than we should like to hear.

For the Porteous affair Scott had plenty of documentary stuff—indeed, the reader who trudges through the 'Magnum'

---

[1] See Grierson, *Sir Walter Scott*, pp. 164-5.

notes may well wish it less.[2] The actual event is admirably fitted for the purpose to which he puts it, having the impact of a crisis—one which brings matters to a head. Moreover, the action is concluded in a matter of days; yet the reverberations continue so long as the novelist chooses to register them. The magnitude and weight are right: what happened during those September days of 1736 in Edinburgh remains memorable—at least in Edinburgh, and Scott is able to persuade us that we must surely have known what it was to be a citizen of 'the good town'. On the other hand, response to the story does not echo down long corridors thronged with ghosts, as in the aftermath of civil war. Nevertheless, it had a significance for the present—Scott's present at least.

The clearest account of the whole transaction as Scott regarded it is to be found in his *Tales of a Grandfather*, where it occupies some twenty-four pages—perhaps a little out of proportion, but, as he announces at the outset, it 'must be simply regarded as a strong and powerful display of the cool, stern, and resolved manner in which the Scottish, even of the lower classes, can concert and execute a vindictive purpose'.[3] But this chronicle of Scotland which he wrote for his grandson is harder to come by than his novels; I therefore extract from it the gist of this episode—one which, however enigmatic, certainly has a beginning, a middle, and an end.

The affair played itself out within a few days and nights, in identifiable parts of Edinburgh, and involved persons known to history, with others whose part in it is on record but not their names. Two men, Andrew Wilson and George Robertson, smugglers by trade, were convicted of breaking into the custom-house to recoup themselves for the loss of confiscated goods, and were sentenced to death. It was a sentence which could not be impugned, but would not be popular. In the second of two attempts, Wilson effected the escape of his accomplice, but remained to pay

---

[2] Scott had a large collection of relevant pamphlets, which he did not trouble to digest, having neither time nor strength for such work when he compiled notes for the 'Magnum' edition of his novels.

[3] Third Series, Vol. II, p. 156.

the penalty.[4] Responsibility for maintaining order at the scene of his execution, about which the civil authorities were apprehensive, was assigned to John Porteous, Captain of the City Guard, supported by regular soldiers.[5] He was a brutal fellow, and used the prisoner with a callousness which shocked that not very tender generation. The large crowd assembled, quiet until Wilson was dead, presently began to show ominous signs of their mood.[6] The 'soldiers' opened fire, and continued until a number of manifestly innocent people had been killed. There was afterwards some doubt as to who had given the fatal order, but a witness testified that Porteous himself had snatched a musket from a 'soldier' and fired it. He was tried for murder and sentenced to death; but a reprieve from London overruled the Edinburgh verdict on the day fixed for his execution, and a pardon was expected to follow. On the night of 7 September 1736 a notably well-organized and even orderly crowd virtually assumed control of Edinburgh: taking the law into their own hands, they broke into the Tolbooth, where Porteous was celebrating his reprieve, and carried him to the customary place of execution, where he was duly hanged. The gathering then quietly dispersed. No one had been injured; even the 'soldiers' were merely disarmed, and the rope had been paid for. Indignation in London, where Queen Caroline was Regent, provoked so intemperate a decree against the whole city of Edinburgh as must have strained the Union. But the Duke of Argyle and Duncan Forbes succeeded in allaying this passion and reducing the penalty to a fine. Despite a rigorous investigation, not one of the persons who had conspired to execute their own judgement on Porteous was ever apprehended. They were said to have worn disguise. Certainly no one could be found

[4] Alexander Caryle denied his altruism; but, although he had been a witness both at Robertson's escape and Wilson's execution, it was many years later that he set down his recollections: *Anecdotes and Characters of the Time*, ed. James Kinsley (1976), p. 18.

[5] Since the City Guards were veterans, they are referred to as soldiers, but I shall distinguish them from the regular troops by inverted commas.

[6] Carlyle asserts that there was no more to it than the usual reaction of the more turbulent spectators after an execution (p. 19). If he is right, the tension between the authorities and the crowd must have been unusually taut.

to inform against them. Many years later, an old man was alleged to have admitted his complicity; but his family denied this.

Scott's handling of material relating to the Porteous affair is not very different from that which he had learned and practised when he was engaged on the historical sources of *Old Mortality*. The records at his disposal for both were numerous, but all much of a kind. Such modifications as he allowed himself (apart from details of time and place) complied with a convention which he had himself established. He would take someone known to have been involved (in the assassination of the Archbishop or the conflict with Porteous), weave him into the broader fabric of his narrative and develop or distort his character and career, according to his subsequent appearances and employment in the novel. But the second of the three stories composing *The Heart of Midlothian* offers a marked contrast in that, whereas both tale and theme were originally simple—the condemnation of a young woman for the alleged murder of her illegitimate child and the heroic exploit by which her sister obtained a 'remission' of the sentence—the sources used by Scott are not easy to unravel.

Very early in 1817, Mrs Goldie, wife of Thomas Goldie, Commissary of Dumfries, sent Scott a 'communication'.[7] This consisted of an account of her meeting, some twenty-six years ago, with Helen Walker, the woman who had saved her sister's life, together with a covering note—neither bearing signature or date. Nor is any mention made of the date of the events recalled.[8] The 'communication'—that is, the information offered to Scott—falls into three distinct parts: first, a description of the Abbey of Lincluden, hard by whose ruins Mrs Goldie had taken lodgings for the summer; secondly, an encounter with an old woman, who, on parting, hesitantly

[7] Manuscript in the University Library of Edinburgh, posted 31 January 1817. I owe the favour of a photostat to the Library.

[8] Grierson says that Scott would be struck by the coincidence of Isobel Walker's case with the Porteous affair. If so, it must have been part of knowledge he already had, or could easily obtain. For the assumption, see Grierson, *Sir Walter Scott*, p. 163. For the long-drawn-out Walker case, stretching from 1736 to 1738, see W. S. Crockett, *The Scott Originals* (1912), discussed below.

admitted that her name was Helen Walker, and referred Mrs Goldie to her husband for the story behind the name; thirdly, that story recounted the same evening by 'Mr —', evidently Thomas Goldie; the whole concluding with Mrs Goldie's wish for further intercourse, which was to be frustrated by Helen's death. The covering note asks that such merit should be commemorated.

The Heart of Midlothian appeared in July 1818[9]—Scott, as usual, making no acknowledgement of his personal debt. By the end of that year, Mrs Goldie (still remaining anonymous) and the editor of *The Dumfries and Galloway Courier*, John M'Diarmid, evidently felt free to publish the 'communication' which, they must suppose, had contributed so much to that novel—in a lightly revised version. This *The Scotsman* reprinted, with due acknowledgement.[10] There the matter rested until, in his Introduction to the first series of *Chronicles of the Canongate* (1827), Scott, having relinquished the pretence of anonymity, spoke of his own indebtedness to 'an unknown correspondent (a lady)' for Helen Walker's story, and praised 'the truth and force of the original sketch, which I regret that I am unable to present to the public, as it is written with much feeling and spirit'.[11] Three years later, in the 'Magnum' edition of the novel, he opened his budget. This contained the original 'communication', and much besides: the name of 'the late' Mrs Goldie, a letter from her daughter with a few further particulars about the Walkers, and a renewal of her mother's plea for a memorial—to which Scott promised to attend. He added a Postscript, containing matter reproduced, not always exactly, from the tale as it had lately been retold by yet another writer. At the beginning of that year, John M'Diarmid had published a little volume of essays: *Sketches from Nature.*[12] The last of these is

---

[9] Grierson, op. cit., p. 165, correcting Lockhart.

[10] J. C. Corson, in his *Bibliography of Sir Walter Scott* (1943), item 1594, enumerates: the article in *The Courier*, which even he has not seen; the reprint in *The Scotsman*, and a reprint from that reprint.

[11] pp. ix-x. Scott was to add his correspondent's name in the 'Magnum' edition of *I Cannongate* in 1832.

[12] 'Printed by John M'Diarmid and Co., Dumfries', published in

called 'The Real Story of Jeanie Deans'.[13] In respect of
Helen's character and reputation it tallies with the accounts
of Mrs Goldie and her daughter. Certain particulars in the
narrative agree rather with the novel than with their recollections, and some are closer to the version in *The Scotsman*
than either. Thus, Helen borrowed money for her journey (as
in the novel); she obtained 'letters of recommendation' (not
unlike the Butler papers in the novel); the pardon, once
granted, was 'despatched to Scotland', and the petitioner,
'after her purse had been replenished, returned home'. Mrs
Goldie's version had been, here as elsewhere, more romantic:
she sends Helen back, carrying the pardon and on foot, to
arrive only just in time. It may be inferred that Scott and
M'Diarmid have the stronger sense of probability.

M'Diarmid does not call his narrative 'the real story of
Helen Walker'; such corrections as he seems to offer are
courteously and discreetly introduced. So are his references
to Scott—unless we hear sardonic overtones in his tribute to
the 'fertile genius' which had expanded the story into 'an
interesting and somewhat bulky novel', and the expressed
hope that, in the forthcoming edition, Mrs Goldie's part will
be duly acknowledged. But it is a matter on which he is
silent that notably, and most strangely, divides M'Diarmid
from both Mrs Goldie and Scott. Whereas she had told how
Helen learned of the charge 'on being called as principal
witness against' her sister, and was informed by the defending counsel that she could save her simply by affirming that
Isobel had made her condition known to her,[14] M'Diarmid
goes no further than this: Helen was told (he does not say by
whom nor in what circumstances) how to deliver her sister—
neither lawyer nor legal process is mentioned. That his
omission of the summons to bear witness cannot be dismissed as negligence is clear from Crockett's statement: in

---

Edinburgh and London; the Preface dated 25 January 1830; the 'real
story' described as hurriedly written. The volume consists of observations on natural history, reflections on local worthies, and obituaries
for *The Dumfries and Galloway Courier*, revised.

[13] pp. 380-8.

[14] Can she really mean that Helen was called by the prosecution and
instructed by the defence?

the records of the trial, 'Helen does not appear on the scene at all.'[15] She was never summoned. Thus, what Mrs Goldie thought she had learned from her husband as to the cruel dilemma in which Helen was placed may have no factual foundation. Its value for Scott is another story, to be considered presently.

I proposed to sift out three historical components in *The Heart of Midlothian*. The third of these is the part played by the Duke of Argyle.[16] Scott had ample material for this in the political history of the troubled years that followed the Union, and in the recollections of his friend, Lady Louisa Stuart, who commanded a remarkable memory. The Duke was a major figure in Scott's historical pantheon: a memorable man, associated (over much of his career) with the championship of Scottish rights. To the casual reader he may seem the means by which Scott connects his two stories, and little besides. He counts for much more than this. If the narrative offered by Mrs Goldie was new to Scott, his attention must have been arrested by a name already associated in his mind with peace-making after the Porteous riot. We can gauge its significance by the care he takes to weave pointed allusions into the early chapters: word goes about that the Duke of Argyle has stood up to Queen Caroline in her wrath, and tempered the excesses of the Council of Regency.[17] This may serve as sufficient preparation for Ratcliffe's advice to Jeanie to seek out MacCallummore.[18] But Scott has a larger purpose. Into that bulky and overloaded chapter which begins with Jeanie's escape from Ratcliffe on Salisbury Crags and ends with Bailie Middleburgh's visit to David Deans (some weeks later), he inserts a succinct account of the political issue: the grave injury and affront offered by the Council of Regency to the city of Edinburgh, notably by its infringement of ecclesiastical independence.[19] The

[15] op. cit., p. 235. He surmises that Helen may have been urged by Isobel's friends to volunteer the required information, but repeats: 'Helen Walker had no summons to the witness-box' (p. 409).

[16] Grierson refers to this: op. cit., pp. 163–4; but his terse statement will bear amplification.

[17] I. 178 and II. 298; Chapters vii and xxiv.

[18] II. 314; Chapter xxv.

[19] II. 155–6; Chapter xviii. Compare the unencumbered account in *Tales of a Grandfather*, Third Series, Vol. II, pp. 173–4.

placing is awkward: the passage follows on the dense court scene, in which Middleburgh has to deal with Staunton's rigmarole-letter and the assaults of Meg Murdockson and her daughter Madge.[20] Nevertheless we need the information if we are to understand the debate between Middleburgh and Deans. The characters of both have been established: that of Deans (which matters more) very fully in the chapter which reaches back into family history:[21] the families of Deans, Butler, and Dumbiedikes are all, one way or another, rooted in the past, and for Deans it is an historical past which governs his thought and conduct in the present. We have become acquainted with his contentiousness; we learn here what he is contentious about. There is a strong undertow in these waters, this confluence of past and present, calling for an experienced navigator.

There must be a peculiar satisfaction for the story-teller, whether he is writing historical fiction or authentic history, in the conjunction of the hour and the man. Here, in two stories, close enough in time for his purpose, Scott found the name of a man fit to mediate between suppliant and sovereign, even in an unpropitious time: the man to whom he would gladly assign such a function. If he owed this auspicious name to Mrs Goldie, he would, for that alone, owe her some gratitude. I wish he had tossed her a morsel of thanks, a mere mention of his 'anonymous correspondent'—before she died.

Historical inspiration, in *The Heart of Midlothian*, is not confined to those three stories. Scott was bent, not only on writing history (whether plain or adorned), but also on living it. In 1818 he was preoccupied with a situation which might prove critical. Here again his theme was respect for rights which should have survived the Union. In the first two months of that year the whereabouts of the Scottish regalia was much in his thoughts. On 14 January he wrote to Morritt of a Commission which had been appointed to open the strong-room in Edinburgh Castle and examine the chest in which the regalia had been deposited: 'There is an odd

---

[20] Had Scott forgotten that he had allowed Madge to escape, with Ratcliffe's connivance, the night before? Here she is again, back in the Tolbooth.

[21] I. 183–203; Chapter viii.

mystery hung about the fate of these royal symbols of national independence. The spirit of the Scotch at the union clung fondly to these emblems and to soothe their jealousy it was specially provided by an article of the union that the regalia should never be removed under any pretext from the Kingdom of Scotland.' Nevertheless there arose a general suspicion 'that the regalia had been sent to London . . .'. A Commission had indeed opened the room, 'fifteen or twenty years ago', and found a reassuring deposit of dust on the chest, but forbore to break it open. Now the room was to be entered and the chest opened.[22] A letter to Croker of 7 February reports the event. All was well; but 'the removal of the Regalia might have greatly irritated people's minds, and offered a fair pretext of breaking the Union, which for thirty years was the predominant wish of the Scottish nation'.[23]

This theme of independence and its symbols is woven into the story, all the way to the true climax, the winning of the pardon. Thus, when Jeanie is confronted with yet another dilemma, posed by Staunton's letter—whether she shall deliver him up as the much wanted 'Robertson'—she reflects that the Porteous riot was a protest against violation of 'the idea of ancient national independence', and that the measures which had followed were keeping indignation alight.[24] These reflections do her less than justice. Like every passage in which George Staunton's voice is heard, it sounds cracked in the ring; but the tenor agrees with Scott's own thought, through all the historical part of the novel.

Independence has many meanings. Divide it broadly into ideal and practical, and within the ideal there are still distinctions. Scott had a deep insight into visions of life and values other than his own, provided they were rooted in history. Those of David Deans have been fostered by a hundred years of Scottish history. Though he repudiates the title of Independent, with its Cromwellian associations, independence of

[22] *Letters*, Grierson, V. 48-9.
[23] ibid., pp. 74-5. See Grierson's note. Lockhart records Scott's deep concern, as remembered by his daughter, who was with him when the chest was reopened on the following day. See *Life*, III. 157-8.
[24] III. 248; Chapter xxxiv.

a peculiar kind is the key to his habits of thought. Rejecting the claims of civil government, he demands, not a theocracy, but *the* theocracy, that belonging to the heirs of the Covenant. For him there can be no authority other than that acknowledged by the true remnant—and therefore none elsewhere than in Scotland. How the rest of the world is to be governed does not appear. He is doubly committed to living in an ideal past: both by his habitual reference to the conduct of the ancient Israelites, as these are represented in some books of the Old Testament, and by his constant resolve to keep faith with the dead, those who suffered for the Covenant. (This is a motive which, even in politics, has more force than the sceptic can understand.)

Scott has been accused of living in the past, because his imagination delighted to dwell in it. Has it ever been observed that those of his characters who conduct their lives as though the past were the true reality come near to destroying what they most cherish in the present, the lives of those they love? Captive to this illusion of an undying past, Deans recognizes no issue but one: whether Jeanie shall bear witness in a court which has for him no validity. What she will have to testify never enters his head. Thus, for all their mutual devotion, these two are helplessly at cross purposes, and her father's permission to make her own decision is cruelly ambiguous. ' "Can this be?" said Jeanie, as the door closed on her father—"Can these be his words that I have heard? . . . A sister's life, and a father pointing out how to save it!" '[25]

All that has gone to make this misunderstanding inevitable was conveyed to us in David's former course and his recent dispute with Middleburgh: the independence which isolates him, forbidding apprehension of any train of thought other than his own. In revealing the grain imposed on character by the pressures of history, Scott is unmatchable. Thus it is clear that Jeanie, nudged, cajoled, and threatened by others, will get neither counsel nor support from her father. She has derived from him her sense of absolute values. The application will rest with her. The law that binds her is moral, invested with religious authority by the oath which she must

[25] II. 187; Chapter xix.

swear. The law in whose meshes she is trapped is civil, and the particular statute under which she is summoned to bear witness has neither morality nor common sense to warrant it. Believing whole-heartedly that her sister is innocent, and having Staunton's evidence as to the abduction of the child, she will be questioned on another matter, and to that question alone she may reply. The outcome of false testimony would be a true verdict; the outcome of her true testimony will be a false verdict. A casuist might resolve this, but we are impelled to cry out with Mrs Saddletree, when her husband expounds the case: ' "If the law makes murders . . . the law should be hanged for them; or if they wad hang a lawyer instead, the country wad find nae faut!" '[26] Perhaps this is why there have been attempts to belittle the issue, criticism even sinking so low as to suggest that there was no dilemma— Jeanie was jealous of her pretty sister.

If there had been no dilemma, Scott would not have written the story. It is important to understand what he received, before observing how his genius transformed it. Mrs Goldie, though her introductory description suggests literary aspirations, was evidently not a practised narrator, nor (despite her husband's profession) very clear about legal procedure. So much the better: a great imagination often works more freely on material which has still to be shaped. As Scott first encountered the story in her 'communication', Helen was called as witness for the prosecution, but was instructed by counsel for the defence how she should answer if she would save her sister. Her answer to this advice is given, but nothing is said of her appearance in court. ' "The trial came on, and the sister was found guilty and condemned" '—that was what Mrs Goldie remembered of her husband's tale, after twenty-six years. It is true that, as the story appeared in *The Scotsman*, the sisters meet in court.[27] But we have here to weigh two possibilities: that, by the end of 1818, Mrs Goldie and M'Diarmid had gathered further particulars; or that they were unconsciously influenced by

---

[26] I. 1 27–8; Chapter v.
[27] 'In removing the prisoner from the bar, she was heard to say "O Nelly! ye hae been the cause o' my death!" Helen replied, "Ye ken I buid to speak the truth." '

the novel—and I think the balance tilts that way. The story asked for a climax in court, and Scott, with his knowledge of legal procedure, was not likely to deny it. Indeed, if he had had no more than a commonplace imagination, he must as a lawyer have made something memorable of this scene. But that very professional knowledge compelled him to find a way round the difficulty in which Mrs Goldie had involved her tale: who was to tell Jeanie of the question she would be asked and the answer she must give? The lawyer defending Effie must not know that she would never give that answer. Scott transferred to Staunton the task of informing her, and out of that expedient developed the situation in the Tolbooth—perhaps the most poignant in the whole story—when Jeanie is betrayed into telling Effie what she has learnt about her own power. (Scott was steering very close to *Measure for Measure* here, as he means us to infer from his chapter-headings.) He has now to ensure that the lawyer defending Effie shall not know how matters stand with his principal witness; so Mr Fairbrother is deputizing for an absent colleague, and all is set for disaster.

What Mrs Goldie gave Scott was an *idea*. If he turned to the records of the case—as he may well have done, once she had drawn his attention to it—he would not find this striking antithesis: the scrupulous witness who will not do what is required of her, but will go to any lengths on another and a harder course, which she judges lawful. Because it fired his imagination, he brought to it all that was needed to make it credible, and understandable: the pressures of history— national and family history—on that mysterious entity, the individual soul.

And here the even more mysterious activity of genius can be perceived, working to fire and fuse the whole. The story gave not only integrity, but also vigour of body and mind— without these it could not have happened. Scott clearly enjoyed framing an appropriate childhood and upbringing. He added something else: simplicity. Helen Walker was 'a wily body'. She was, moreover, when Mrs Goldie met her,[28]

[28] When John M'Diarmid sought information about her, there were those who could remember her, but none who could have known her when young.

an old woman, charged with memories she did not wish to
share. Scott had to create Jeanie; and it was an extraordinary
achievement. Simplicity of character poses peculiar problems
for the novelist or dramatist. I do not mean the delineation
of characters simply conceived, as in popular fiction—black
or white. I am thinking of characters conceived as simple:
unworldly, looking out on our complicated world with the
singleness of vision enjoined on us by the Gospel, and therefore widely separated from the story-teller, whose imagination must be complex if he is to enter into diverse states of
mind and heart. The practice of the English novelists suggests
that this is almost impossible, except in conjunction with
weakness—the natural, innocent weakness of childhood or
old age. Jeanie Deans stands alone. To create and to sustain
are, however, distinct functions. Scott is able to sustain this
impression of steadfast simplicity and strength not only
throughout the trial, but also in the two nicely juxtaposed
scenes of courtship that are precipitated by Jeanie's deter-
mination to set out for London. He surely wavers on the
journey—if only in the Willingham episode. Whenever George
Staunton appears, probity vanishes. His very language is, to
borrow Jane Austen's words, 'such thorough novel slang—
and so old, that I dare say Adam met with it in the first novel
he opened'.[29] Even the explanation of his behaviour, most
improbably offered to Jeanie by a Staunton family servant
as she rides pillion behind him, is a mere commonplace of the
nineteenth-century novel: he was born in the West Indies—
the East Indies will do. Scott tried to defend him;[30] but he
is indefensible. We have only to compare his cascade of reproaches to Jeanie on Salisbury Crags with Effie's terrible
home-thrust: ' "Ye'll have time to repent." '[31]

The Willingham episode is, however, merely the most un-
satisfactory part of the journey to London; and all of that is
questionable. Scott had, in his source, the plain, arduous,

---

[29] *Letters*, ed. R. W. Chapman (1832), Letter 101.
[30] *Letters*, Grierson, V. 67; to James Ballantyne, 1818.
[31] II. 208; Chapter xx. M'Diarmid gives the words, assigning them to
nameless friends of Isobel Walker. The reproach may have been part of
the traditional story, but only Scott could have found those words for
it. The 'True Story' is unconsciously echoing the novel.

and perhaps monotonous two weeks' travel, on foot. He sub-
stituted for it a succession of hindrances and furtherances:
Jeanie is tossed to and fro between the Murdocksons on the
one hand, and, on the other, the Stauntons and casual well-
wishers. When Scott tucks her into the Stamford coach, her
travail is ended: the real difficulties of finding Mrs Glass and
presenting herself to the Duke of Argyle are impatiently
passed over. This version of the heroic journey is radically
unworthy of the original. The coincidences are of course outrageous. Moreover, Jeanie is too heavily taxed as communi-
cator and interpreter. She must catch the upshot of thieves'
slang through a chink in her prison wall, and from this and
Madge's obscure hints infer almost the whole of the Murdockson story, with its bearing on her own quest.[32] She
must read yet another of George Staunton's canting letters as
she rides pillion behind his father's groom, and gather the
rest of the Staunton story from the man's talk.[33] Improbability is in itself no insuperable bar to enjoyment, but there is
something here that alienates more irrevocably than un-
likelihood can do. Such melodramatic nonsense is an affront
to the tragic issue of that story of the two sisters. Tragedy,
we know, does not require the death of a protagonist; but
with some of its demands the story-teller who undertakes it
must comply. Seriousness is necessary—and nothing can be
less serious than melodrama, unless it is the next-of-kin,
farce. To draw towards finer distinctions—that, for example,
between tragedy and romance: for tragedy it is indispensable
that we should feel 'Nothing will ever be the same again.'
The symbol of romance is the circle, or ring—completed or
mended at the close. What is broken, in tragedy, is gone
for ever.

Nothing will ever be the same again—that is the tragic
implication of what befalls the family, alike in *The Heart of
Midlothian* and *The Master of Ballantrae*. David and Jeanie
Deans both recognize this, though Scott—having, as a novelist,
happiness in his gift—will presently bestow oblivion on them.
That is part of the romantic ending which so clearly belongs
to another story. But the journey to London, however

---

[32] III. 112–20; Chapter xxx.
[33] III. 250–4; Chapter xxxiv.

accomplished, is the very heart of this tale of the two sisters. Provided only that Scott sustains the sense of heroic exploit, does it matter how? Imaginative literature (I reply) admits this paradox: it is possible to diminish by addition. When Scott adds those adventures on the road, he takes something from the tragic intensity of the family situation. So does Stevenson, when he launches into the Master's adventures after Culloden. Power has to be generated afresh, on his return to Durrisdeer, Jeanie's arrival in London. It is true that the impulse to foist these hazards into the two novels need not be attributed to expediency alone, though Scott (for one) was fatally committed to expansion. The theme of flight and pursuit has an irresistible attraction, for the story-teller as well as the reader. We are often bound to confess that we 'could not put the book down'. He, we may suspect, could not stop inventing and circumventing hazards. So much the worse: we are all too willingly seduced.

For Scott's deviation from the original tale of the journey to London I offer no defence; but his handling of the way in which the petition was obtained is quite another matter. Mrs Goldie's version is pure fairy-tale: Helen Walker 'with her simple (perhaps ill-expressed) petition, drawn up by some inferior clerk of the court . . . presented herself, in her tartan plaid and country attire, to the late Duke of Argyle, who immediately procured the pardon she petitioned for'. This easy magic was too insubstantial for those two characters, Jeanie and the Duke, as Scott had conceived them. Besides, he had in his gift something better—bolder, yet more authentic. What he gave to the story was historical insight and knowledge of the whole situation—together with something peculiarly his own. His mastery of vernacular dialogue allows it to rise to the occasion. The means by which he brings all this into play deserves attention. Jeanie's first encounter with the Duke is an affair of plain prose. The emphasis falls throughout on her good sense and quiet behaviour, with hardly a hint of the eloquence that would presently be needed. To engage the Duke's active support, Scott resorts to his favourite theme of a good turn requited, and calls up an episode in the career of Reuben Butler's grandfather—who has changed from Stephen to Benjamin, but Scott was often

careless about names—and the Duke honours this questionable obligation. Helen Walker had brought with her a written
petition; Reuben Butler is again employed, and even Bartoline
Saddletree and a speedy postal service, in furnishing Jeanie
with papers bearing on her sister's case. So far, the resources
of the practised romantic novelist will serve. But it is the hard
fact of the historical situation which calls into action Scott's
true genius. The Duke's protest that he lacks influence is no
mere formality; he was then doubly disadvantaged, both as
the opponent of the Queen's ally, Sir Robert Walpole, and
the man who had withstood those harsh measures which
expressed her anger at the Porteous riots and the immunity
of the rioters. Drawing on his knowledge of Horace Walpole's
Reminiscences,[34] and doubtless familiar, from his work on
Swift, with the interplay of court and government at that
time, Scott constructed a taut, well sprung, one-act play.

I take issue here with Mr Cockshut, maintaining that his
book[35] suffers from the limitation of scope he imposed on
himself: Scott as historian, commentator on the historical
ballads in the *Minstrelsy*, author of *Tales of a Grandfather*,
editor of Dryden and Swift, is injuriously neglected. That (I
believe) is why Mr Cockshut is shocked to discover in this
episode 'a strange political world, which might certainly be
described as cynical'.[36] Admittedly, the pleasantries offend;
but I doubt whether Mary Berry, if she had come on their
like in editing the *Reminiscences*, would have excised them;
to every age its own indelicacies; and these are merely incidental. The dramatic tension—not incompatible with
an issue of life or death—derives from sustained uncertain-
ties. The Duke is taking a calculated risk. The Queen,
steering between the rocks of political fact and the shallows
of political fiction, seems prepared only to conciliate the
Duke by granting an interview at which she will condescend
to explain her refusal of a pardon. Jeanie is moving in a
world of incalculable possibilities—she may be the least
surprised of the three at the outcome. Of course it is a

[34] Acknowledged in the 'Magnum'. Scott possessed the 1798 *Works*,
and would find what he needed in the fourth volume.
[35] A. O. J. Cockshut, *The Achievement of Walter Scott* (1969).
[36] op. cit., p. 186.

political world—the world of George II, and not of Haroun
al Raschid.

That outcome is admirably designed. Jeanie, her father's
daughter, is able to fend off the Queen's first question:
whether she 'had any friends engaged in the Porteous mob?'
But the hypothetical rider—'If you were possessed of such
a secret, you would hold it matter of conscience to keep it
to yourself?'[37]—baffles her; for this is at the very heart of
the story. George Staunton's worthless life is in the keeping
of three women, and safe from the law's reach, though not
one of them has any power or even security. Two, Effie and
Madge, guard it because they are infatuated with him; but for
Jeanie it is a matter of conscience. Each may say: a man's
life is in my hands, and it is not for sale. But the motive is
not the same. The Queen's shot goes home, and Jeanie's
answer, though true to her upbringing, seems to give the
advantage to her sceptical adversary:

'I would pray to be directed and guided what was the line of
duty, madam', answered Jeanie.
'Yes, and take that which suited your own inclinations',
replied her Majesty'.

Now, when all seems lost, comes the turning-point. For the
Queen's questions (which are merely tactical) have cost her
the strategic victory. By linking the two cases she has brought
vehemently into Jeanie's mind the contrast: Porteous, gone
to his account, where he may have much to answer; her
sister, awaiting death for a crime of which she is not guilty;
and her tongue is loosed. When she can speak no more, the
Queen turns to the Duke of Argyle with the words: ' "This
is eloquence." ' She is right: it is a passage at which envy
alone can cavil. While perfectly apt to the speaker and the
occasion—justifying Scott's plan of reserving Jeanie's plea
for an appeal to another woman—it transcends both.[38]

And then the author proceeds to diminish by addition.
Helen Walker had returned as she had come, and died alone

---

[37] III. 324; Chapter xxxvii.
[38] ' "When the hour of death comes, that comes to high and low—
long and late may it be yours" '—is the reader expected to recall that
Caroline was to die in the following year?

and poor. Scott was under no obligation to follow to its close a story which he had already amplified and altered to suit the purposes of fiction. But what he now adds impairs all that has gone before: it is false to tragic tone and historical context. His generous heart, his pleasure in giving satisfaction to his readers, and the necessity he had incurred of filling a fourth volume, committed Scott to a process of belittlement. The happy ending[39] on which he was bent makes light of the breach within the family; the Duke of Argyle, as its agent, shrinks to a fairy godfather. Amidst all these changes, the vision which has been at the heart of the story fades. David Deans, displaced from his Lowland habitation, and subdued to these new demands of comedy, loses the historical significance for which he had formerly been memorable—and with it, his integrity: he temporizes, and looks to the main chance. Jeanie is robbed of her strength and simplicity. Did any other novelist throw away so much as Scott? Had any other so much to throw away?

There must surely be something precarious in the circumstances of the historical novelist, something not unlike that which Shelley discerns in the poet's situation.

The mind in creation is as a fading coal, which some invisible influence, like an inconstant wind, awakes to transitory brightness . . . . Could this influence be durable in its original purity and force, it is impossible to predict the greatness of the results; but when composition begins, inspiration is already on the decline . . .[40]

It may at first glance seem eccentric to associate these two, the poet and one particular kind of prose narrator. Is not the writer whose inspiration springs from the past more securely planted than his fellow novelists, furnished as he is with documentary stuff? One uncertainty they share, if their work is greatly imagined: they have to reckon with what Kipling called his daemon—with the sense of a power coming they know not whence, and therefore unlikely to be renewed at their bidding. Scott's talk of his magic wand and Stevenson's

---

[39] Happy only for the deserving; but what happiness are they supposed to enjoy alone?

[40] *A Defence of Poetry*, ed. H. F. B. Brett-Smith (1929), pp. 53–4.

insistence on the validity of his dreams point the same way. Nevertheless there seems to be an evanescence peculiar to the vision soliciting the imagination of the story-teller whose traffic is with the past. The brighter its flame, the sooner it burns out. It may last long enough for a short story. Try to sustain it beyond its proper duration, and the result is likely to be a novel which we could wish unfinished. Or, even if left unfinished, it may provoke the wish that the author had not told us how he meant to finish it. The discovery of a letter from Jane Austen, disclosing how she meant to proceed with *Sanditon*, would be simply a gratified wish: nothing can shake our belief that it was *all there*. Why then can we not accept thankfully those letters about the future course of *Weir of Hermiston*?

For Stevenson, inspiration would always ebb and flow with the fluctuations in his bodily strength; it was therefore his custom to turn from one story to another, as though hoping to make headway elsewhere. Thus he left several fragments, of which one, *Heathercat*, asks to be compared with *Weir of Hermiston*. It likewise derives from his pre-occupation as an exile with 'that cold old huddle of grey hills' from which he came.[41] It reaches further back into Scottish history, and promises to challenge *Old Mortality* on its own ground. It was to have been called *The Killing Time*.[42] Stevenson had formerly read much, and now intended to read more, about the successive waves of dissidence in the south-west of Scotland, towards the end of the seventeenth century. This was to be 'an attempt at a real historical novel', such as would 'present a whole field of time; the race —our own race—the west land and Clydesdale blue bonnets, under the influence of their last trial, when they got to a pitch of organisation in madness that no other peasantry has ever made an offer at'.[43] Scott had been likewise impressed by the spontaneous order of the Porteous mob, but

---

[41] *Letters*, Colvin, IV. 122; to J. M. Barrie from Vailima, 1 Nov. 1892.

[42] ibid., p. 269; to R. A. M. Stevenson from Vailima, 17 June 1894.

[43] From the same letter, p. 268. 'Our own race', because he was writing to his cousin, and referring to the region from which he supposed their ancestors to derive.

sacrificed the impression to the plot and George Staunton. The story of *Heathercat*—that is, the predicament of particular characters—was to be drawn from legal records—'Fountainhall', as usual, affording matter. The opening situation is clear: antagonism within a family, caused by civil strife. Stevenson could, but need not, have recalled one of Scott's notes on a Covenanting ballad, 'The Battle of Bothwell Bridge', in the third (1803) volume of his *Minstrelsy of the Scottish Border*, where he quotes Fountainhall on the plight of men who pleaded that they had neglected the royal summons only from 'apprehension of disquiet from their wives'. Despite Scott's reassuring presence, a firm historical basis, and Stevenson's own long-standing interest in the historical setting, *Heathercat* seems to be little regarded. Can the objection be that which Stevenson himself alleges against *The Master of Ballantrae*: lack of 'pleasurableness'?[44] It is true that the exploitation of the boy, Francis Traquair, by his termagant mother, in defiance of his broken-spirited father, is painful to contemplate; but who cares about that, now? Then, place and time are remote, and spontaneous popular uprising may lack for us the charm it held for Stevenson, and Scott. Indeed, Stevenson himself admitted that he found Scottish history in the last decade of the seventeenth century 'obscure'.[45] Nevertheless, he makes the situation plain, and, even in the space of three and a half chapters, four or five characters emerge distinctly. Therefore I must suppose that *Heathercat* has suffered eclipse by the far greater brilliance of *Weir of Hermiston*.

It is generally agreed that this would have been Stevenson's masterpiece, but two obstacles to understanding have to be recognized. The first is a question posed by Sidney Colvin, and still unanswered: why did Stevenson, having explicitly and emphatically chosen Braxfield for his model, change the date? Braxfield, Colvin objects, was notorious in his own day and a legend afterwards; but that day was the end of the eighteenth century, and Stevenson opens his story in the second dacade of the nineteenth—by which time his behaviour

[44] *Letters*, Colvin, IV. 108; to Colvin from Vailima, 30 Sept. 1892.
[45] *Letters to Baxter*, p. 341; from Vailima, 6 Dec. 1893, asking C.B. for documentary matter and information.

was 'somewhat of an anachronism'.[46] So is the lawlessness of the Elliotts. But that is not the whole extent of the damage: Stevenson had originally been drawn to speculate on Braxfield by his portrait (surely flattering?) in a Raeburn exhibition, and essayed a verbal 'character' in *Some Portraits by Raeburn*,[47] fourteen years before he opened to Graham Balfour his plans for *Weir of Hermiston*.[48] In that essay he makes the most of Braxfield's intrepidity in stemming turbulence generated by the French Revolution, ascribing to him disregard for his own safety. Take this away—since it would be meaningless in 1813[49]—and what remains? The trial, presumably representative, of a miserable wretch, for a crime unspecified—conducted with a ferocity which we are meant to recognize as habitual. Yet not only Archie, in revulsion from his own impetuous conduct, but also Lord Glenalmond, venerable and unimpassioned, testifies to a greatness in Lord Hermiston for which there has been *no occasion*. Only a single curious reference may suggest that Stevenson had still at the back of his mind the political context of the original tale, dependent as that must have been on his former impression of Braxfield. When Archie proposed to his father that he should enter the army, Adam Weir upbraided him with being 'Frenchified',[50] though of this there has been no intimation. Indeed, it is hard to reconcile with that allusion to Wellington in the Peninsula, by which we are reminded of the date. It seems that at some point Stevenson had changed his mind as to the historical context. Can this have resulted from his design for the further development of the story?

One question must tingle in the mind of every reader: how, when, and why did Stevenson come to frame a happy

[46] Editorial Note, Edinburgh edition, VII. 302. Braxfield seems to have been an anachronism in his own day, brutal and overbearing by its standards. See W. D. Lyell, *The Real Weir of Hermiston, Robert Macqueen, Lord Braxfield: an Address delivered to the Glasgow Judicial Society* . . . (1903).

[47] *Cornhill Magazine*, July 1878; Edinburgh edition, Vol. III.

[48] *Life*, II. 141-2.

[49] *sic*, in Chapter iii; elsewhere 1812 (*Letters*, Colvin, IV. 119; to Colvin from Vailima, Oct.-Nov. 1892); 1814 (ibid., 146; to Colvin [from Vailima], 30 Jan. 1893.

[50] Chapter iii. Archie admits to former French sympathies, which seem to have left no trace in the text.

ending for a story so deeply tragic in tone? When he died, suddenly and in the very midst of work on *Weir of Hermiston*, he left behind him several accounts of the course he meant it to take. This does not signify prescience: he was sharing hopes and plans with friends, as he had done at the beginning of *The Master of Ballantrae*—and here again curiosity remains only half satisfied. The progress of the work can be traced. In the autumn of 1892 he showed the opening chapters to Graham Balfour, then visiting him at Vailima.[51] By 28 October he is sending Colvin proposals for a title and a list of the characters in 'my new novel'. Neither Glenalmond nor Glenkindie is included; Frank Innes is 'Patrick', and there is an unnamed Lord Justice General. The setting is Edinburgh and the Lammermuirs. Braxfield is mentioned as 'original' for Adam Weir.[52] Three days later he is writing very fully to J. M. Barrie about this third novel he has undertaken, with two already on his hands, and propounding a curious theory. He thanks Barrie for giving a happy ending to *The Little Minister*, although it 'ought to have ended badly; we all know it did'. (Can this be a gentle reference to the prolonged, and—as it turns out—premature obsequies of the hero?) 'If you are going to make a book end badly, it must end badly from the beginning'—as *Richard Feverel* does not. And now he wheels upon his own current work:

I have had a heavy case of conscience of the same kind about my Braxfield story. Braxfield—only his name is Hermiston—has a son who is condemned to death; plainly, there is a fine tempting fitness about this; and I meant he was to hang. But now on considering my minor characters, I saw there were five people who would—in a sense who must—break prison and attempt his rescue. They were capable, hardy folks, too, who might very well succeed. Why should they not then?[53]

---

[51] *Life*, II. 141-2. Balfour likens the pressure of excitement under which Stevenson was writing to that he had experienced when he began *The Master of Ballantrae*.

[52] *Letters*, Colvin, IV. 118-19; from Vailima. I borrow the word 'original' from Scott criticism. Stevenson does not use it.

[53] ibid., pp. 122-4; from Vailima. Quoted by Colvin in his Editorial Note to *Weir of Hermiston*, Edinburgh edition, Vol. VII.

A month later he is writing to Charles Baxter about a more stubborn problem than the means of rescue, though he hopes to solve that by arranging that the case shall not reach Edinburgh. There is mention, as in the letter to Colvin, of the Lord Justice General.[54] We may fairly infer that Stevenson's original vision had been tragic, but not historical: fit, perhaps, for a Jacobean tragedy set in one of those lawless foreign countries, but not for a novel set in historic Scotland. Scottish legal procedure would not allow a father to try his son.

1893 was a bad year for Stevenson. Through sickness, distractions, and anxieties, his letters carry references to revision and even recasting of what has already been drafted,[55] but none to progress. Then, late in 1894, wearying of *St. Ives* which was designed as a mere necessary pot-boiler, he took up *Weir of Hermiston* afresh. Two references in the beginning of December bear witness to his continuing interest in Braxfield—or rather, Raeburn's Braxfield—and his preoccupation with another character whose importance seems to be growing: the elder Kirstie.[56] Two days later he died.

Isobel Strong testified, as his amanuensis and literary confidante, to the exhilaration and confidence with which Stevenson had been working in those last days; the vigour with which the later chapters sustain the momentum of the earlier confirms her report. She left an account of his plan for the rest of the novel. To sum up an intricate plot—doubtless familiar to readers from the version Colvin gave in his Note[57]—Archie was to stand trial before his father for the killing of Frank Innes, who had seduced young Kirstie; to be condemned to death but rescued by her brothers when they learned the truth of his dealings with her. Adam Weir however was to die of the shock. Did Isobel Strong never fully understand the impossibility of this trial of a son by his father on a capital charge, or had Stevenson come to believe that he had somehow circumvented the insuperable difficulty? She would know nothing of Scottish law. He,

[54] *Letters to Baxter*, pp. 313–15; from Vailima.
[55] e.g. *Letters*, Colvin, IV. 143; to Colvin [from Vailima], Jan. 1893.
[56] ibid., pp. 324–5; to Edmund Gosse, 1 Dec. 1894.
[57] Her account (he says) was 'nearly as follows'.

despite his powerful evocation of the world into which he was born, seems to have fallen out of touch with its legal procedure.[58] Perhaps he hoped that he had found a way round the obstacle by the introduction of that shadowy Lord Justice General; but Colvin, looking into this supposition, was advised that it would not work. To another question—where did the break come between the 1892 and the 1894 chapters—the reader is prompted to offer a conjectural answer: continuity is broken when Archie is left, at the close of Chapter IV, explaining himself to Glenalmond and Glenkindie, but found, when Chapter V opens, already installed at Hermiston. True, Stevenson had written to Henry James[59] of *three* chapters drafted before the end of 1893; but he may well have been reckoning only those which were complete.

To these various pieces of evidence we may add the Introductory, remembering that an introduction is not necessarily the first part of a work to be set down in writing. This seems to shift the emphasis from Edinburgh to Hermiston and the younger characters: Frank is to perish, and the Justice-Clerk's son to survive but 'vanish from men's knowledge'.

From this fragmentary evidence and Colvin's commentary it appears that the survival of Archie, though an afterthought, was not a mere belated expedient. But what was Stevenson's real motive for the change? Was it, as he told Barrie, simply concern for the reader's comfort of mind? He had formerly theorized about the obligation to please; now he faced the necessity.[60] After all, 'unless needs must, we have no right to pain our readers.' But then the story should not have been allowed to head towards tragedy.[61] And that is what *Weir of Hermiston* indubitably does. At its very heart is the tragic antagonism between father and son.

And so my argument comes round to the question which I

[58] Stevenson admitted to Baxter that he had played fast and loose with legal propriety in the end of *Kidnapped*; but Rankeillor's trick is in keeping with the temper of the story. See *Letters to Baxter*, p. 168; from Bournemouth end of July 1886.

[59] *James and Stevenson*, p. 217; from Vailima, 5 Dec. 1892.

[60] 'The first duty is to try to feed my family; it is only the second to publish chefs d'oeuvres.' *Letters to Baxter*, p. 371; from Vailima, 4 Nov. 1894.

[61] Letter to Barrie, cited above.

opened and left ajar in the previous chapter: what exactly is the relationship between Stevenson's own experience and the bitter core of *Weir of Hermiston*? Any identification of the persons in these two stories is fallacious: Thomas Stevenson is not Adam Weir, and the differences between him and Robert Louis are not those which alienated Archie from his father. Bearing this in mind, together with all that Stevenson himself wrote about his father, from his death onwards, I can go no further than Sidney Colvin when he writes: 'The difficulties often attending the relation of father and son in actual life had pressed heavily on Stevenson's mind and conscience from the days of his youth, when in obeying the law of his own nature he had been constrained to disappoint, distress, and for a time to be much misunderstood by, a father whom he justly loved and admired with all his heart.'[62] This, while it cannot be extended, may be a little amplified: among the many sorts of tension, and even anguish, inherent in personal relationships, he would, as an only child in a family depleted of children, have a poignant insight into those between father and son. But a story-teller who could imagine the tragic predicament of the elder Kirstie would not stand in need of experience.

In attempting to understand *Weir of Hermiston*, there is one further consideration to be reckoned with. Has it ever been recognized how often, and to what good effect, the hero of an historical novel is *in* the past, but not *of* it? This does not mean that we are to regard him as our contemporary, though he may be credited with some of the insights and sensibilities we claim as ours. It means that circumstances force him, events fling him, into a world which belongs further back than his own. The simplest—even crudest— example is Frank Osbaldiston, the good-for-nothing son who is content merely to enjoy what his father has laboured to win, and is sent to his cousins in the country to learn sense. There he finds himself in an archaic society, and is presently plunged still further back by his association with Rob Roy. Stevenson's *preparing of the generations* is surer and more subtle, the inevitability of the *dark drama* unquestionable.

[62] Editorial Note to *Weir of Hermiston*,

We do not need the murder and trial which he projected to tell us that nothing will ever be the same again, once father and son are brought into judgement on one another. Two historical insights—one into legal society in the Edinburgh of that former age, the other into an even more remote manner of life in the Lammermuirs—have given to it a visionary certitude.

I do not of course suggest that Stevenson was influenced by the regression into a primitive past of Frank Osbaldiston or Edward Waverley, or even his own David Balfour. There is such a factor as natural appropriateness, or convenience. As Johnson observed in the Highlands, it is the traveller rather than the denizen who can tell us how and why that way of life differs from ours. These travellers in time afford a channel of communication: Kirstie's tales of former Elliotts must be told to a listener who is one generation nearer to us than she is; through him we become aware of differences which she would take for granted. And at the last there remains for this captive listener (according to the rules in this game of fiction, and therefore to the scope of our expectation) the possibility of survival, as though by Noah's Ark. He, and such other characters as the story-teller may choose, escape the general calamity, and find refuge in a world not altogether unlike our own. Perhaps it was on Archie's account that Stevenson tampered with dates. A happy ending—if exile with the younger Kirstie can be so regarded—suits better with the second decade of the nineteenth century than the last of the eighteenth. What it does not suit with is the tragic tenor of the story. The spirit of tragedy, in that sombre historical setting, is not to be appeased merely by the death of Adam Weir—nor even of the whole 'giant race before the flood'.

So we come back to the advice Stevenson had given Barrie—'If you are going to make a book end badly, it must end badly from the beginning'[63]—with the clearly implied corollary that one which has been from the first tragic in temper will not bear a happy ending. Yet it was in that same letter that he had declared his intention of contriving such an ending for *Weir of Hermiston*. This, moreover, was in the

---

[63] *Letters*, Colvin, IV. 122-4; cited above.

elation and confidence of 1892; and, even if the initial vision faded in the depression of 1893, it was to be exuberantly renewed in those last weeks of 1894. With that renewal, however, would come a reaffirmation of the resolve to betray it.

I find this inexplicable; but a conviction persists that the fragment we possess of *Weir of Hermiston* is greater than the whole could ever have been—just as the first three volumes of *The Heart of Midlothian* are greater than the four of which it is composed. The poets themselves have been so bold as to suggest that the intrusion of a *person from Porlock* may not always be altogether unwelcome.[64] But then it is necessary that the writer on whom he intrudes should stay behind to tell us how glorious a vision we have lost through his disturbance. Unhappily, that intruder at Vailima came from further off, and did not go away.

[64] e.g. Robert Graves, 'The Person from Porlock' (*More Poems* (1961)).

Chapter V

The Historical Event that Never Happened: *Redgauntlet*, *Esmond*, and *The Tree of Justice*, and some lines by Shakespeare.

To distinguish between historical fiction and fictitious history is not merely to play with terms. There is a particular kind of imagined history which prompts, more urgently than any of the varieties of historical fiction which I have hitherto considered, questions about the working of the imagination, when that strange faculty searches the past. I have tried to show, by means of some few examples, that it may be properly and happily employed in telling stories about people who must have lived—they or their like—though we have no certain knowledge of them, because history has not had occasion to record their lives. It may be shown impinging on them: the story-teller may bring them within the orbit of persons and events known to history, though he had better not claim that those encounters were in any way responsible for what is known to have happened. It is not impossible to extend this licence and allow these imaginary witnesses to fill in some dark interstice: to offer tales about those historical figures which may be supposed to have escaped the historian's notice—provided these do not run counter to what he has to tell us. But there is now a frontier to be crossed: we are to entertain conjectures of events which could not possibly have befallen the historical characters to whom they are attributed.

Shakespeare is probably responsible for almost every licence claimed, and cherished, by the writers of English historical fiction. The presence of Margaret of Anjou in his *Richard III* affords a simple illustration of the freedom to which he considered himself entitled: one of the chorus of wailing, widowed queens, she was in fact an exile in France at the time of her first appearance in the play, and dead before the second. Thus time and place are flouted for the sake of one more queen in that distressful choir.

A more important purpose is served by that comparable violation of time in *Richard II*—comparable, because here again the dramatist is concerned with function rather than character: Richard must have a mourning queen to accompany his downfall. And here I find it significant that Samuel Daniel, that grave, conscientious historian, feeling the same need, should take the same bold measure, turning the 10 year-old Isabella into a grown woman.[1] The relationship between Shakespeare's play and Daniel's poem, complicated by Daniel's revision of his work, is not here relevant: what matters is that both were conscious of the same aesthetic problem. A sense of fitness compelled them to find a woman where none was. Shakespeare's Isabella performs her function, overhearing the gardener's parable of the neglected kingdom and responding antiphonally to Richard's laments.[2] Daniel cannot match this music, but he brings to the relationship between husband and wife a quickness of sympathetic invention such as we expect to find in Shakespeare's fictions: his queen, watching the procession into London after Richard's surrender, assumes the most splendidly mounted figure to be her king, and is dismayed and remoseful when she discovers him to be Bolingbroke. Afraid to look further, she nevertheless finds her eyes drawn to a forlorn and beggarly rider,

Knowing, yet striving not to know 'twas hee,

until Richard, moved by some mysterious sympathy, looks up to the window where she stands concealed.[3]

Shakespeare has a more cogent reason for shuffling the generations, and so bringing onto an even footing those whom differences of age would in fact have kept apart, when he comes to *1 Henry IV*. Whereas his queens have served to

---

[1] Married at 7 years old, she was 10 at the time of Richard's deposition.

[2] III. iv, and V. i.

[3] *The Civil Wars*, Book II, stanzas 66-79; ed. Laurence Minot (Yale, 1958), pp. 117-20.

comment on events in the manner of a Chorus, he now requires not onlookers but contestants: rival champions. Hence his 'young' Hotspur, to match his Prince, and hence their single combat at Shrewsbury. Something may be learnt, here, about the singularity of what I have called fictitious history, and the need for giving it separate consideration. Whereas critical events, vouched for by the historian, may impinge on the lives of those imaginary characters in historical fiction, such crisis makes the theme of fictitious history. Impatient of the gradual process recognized by historians, these writers propose to show us the very point at which the tide turned. And, if that is short of the expected high-water mark, anti-climax can itself be crucial. Where a crown is to be lost, let it be by the narrowest possible margin. Above all, where there is rivalry, let the rivals contend in person, not at long range through intermediaries. For Schiller, Mary Stuart and Elizabeth Tudor must come face to face. Fictitious history gives more, and asks more, than historical fiction: it gives visionary insight into what might have been, what very nearly was. It asks unconditional suspension of disbelief.

Redgauntlet shows that these two kinds of story-telling can be complementary, interwoven within a single novel. Here are the customary characters of fiction, whom the crisis first captures and then, by proving an anti-climax, sets free; but that event could never have happened. To bring it about, Scott has to play fast and loose with chronology. His fiction requires one time-scheme—history, another. Bent on reconciling them, not only for the sake of his story but also in fulfilment of a larger purpose, he draws upon the hard-won cunning of half a lifetime.

It is indispensable to the ravelling and unravelling of the plot in *Redgauntlet* that Darsie should not know, at the outset, anything of the father he has lost, nor how he came to be orphaned. It is natural that his coming of age should impel him to seek an explanation of his apparently kinless state. This, when the truth comes to light, will of course establish the date of the story. There is a contrast to be remarked between the initial impression of vagueness as to when these things happened and a later precision of reference. The letters

of Darsie and Alan bear no dates. They convey an impression
easier to recognize than define, of the Edinburgh of Scott's
youth, in which (according to a later note[4]) the original of
Peter Peebles played a conspicuous part. But these young
men have less sense of history than Scott himself then
possessed: for them, the Union, Rob Roy, and the '45 are
equally remote. The distance is casually measured by Darsie's
surmise that 'Herries of Birrenswork' must be 'one of those
fanatical Jacobites' who had disturbed the peace 'not twenty
years since'.[5] That, for him, is the historic past. He has to
learn that 'Herries' (Hugh Redgauntlet) means to relive
history and change its course. It is not until Scott has relinquished the pretence of letters and journal and taken up the
tale himself that time-references are vouchsafed—for our
benefit. Provost Crosbie's talk of unrest in 'the colonies' and
the consequences of the Stamp Act,[6] to which Alan, fretting
for news of Darsie, pays little attention, adroitly conveys the
information that we are in the year 1765.

Darsie's enlightenment takes a very long while. In possession
of a mystery, Scott is like a dog with a favourite bone: he
cannot let go. Darsie begins to suspect that he may himself
be descended from 'that unhappy race', the Redgauntlets;[7]
but it takes the full length of a tedious misunderstanding,
and understanding, with Lilias to inform him of what has
long been clear to the reader. His attitude remains impersonal:
when he comes to remonstrate with his uncle on the hope-
lessness of the Jacobite cause, he rests his argument on the
difficulty of disturbing 'a dynasty now established for three
reigns'.[8] This is rational, but the time span is also that which
reaches back to his father's death—about which he asks no
questions, nor shows any feeling.

Presently, as Darsie fades into insignificance, the references

[4] Note in the 'Magnum' to Letter xiii. References in *Redgauntlet* are
particularly tiresome. Numbering of chapters begins where the convention of the novel-in-letters breaks down—but these 'chapters' include
instalments of Darsie's journal as well as direct narrative.

[5] II. 162; Chapter viii. Darsie himself has no foothold in time; his
talk of landscape gardening shows Scott failing (for once) to think historically, even when 'Landseer' is corrected to Dodsley. See I. 153,
Letter vii.

[6] II. 246, 259; Chapter xii.   [7] II. 177; Chapter viii.

[8] III. 170; Chapter xii.

to that interval develop a new force, and *twenty years* comes to sound like a knell. It is twenty years since the landing at Moidart;[9] the Prince is not the man he was twenty years ago.[10] For the irony of the situation consists in this—that, whereas the conspirators see their venture as having misfired by a few hours, it is indeed twenty years too late. And yet that passage of twenty years is historically impossible.[11] Not only is there no recorded visit of Charles Edward to Britain in 1765—nor for some years before that; it could not have happened; he was too far in decline. The man who, even in disguise, impresses the reluctant Alan Fairford with a sense of authority was long gone. Scott stretches impossibility further: the mysterious lady whom we are clearly meant to recognize as Clementina Walkinshaw had parted from Charles Edward five years earlier, and could no longer bear responsibility for the divided counsels of his followers—cause of that seemingly fatal delay.

Here, then, is historical fiction, of a kind which Scott has already made familiar and therefore understandable, allied, not with history, but with the manifestly unhistorical—what could never have happened. It seems worth while to ask why: what was to be gained by such a flight of imagination? What, in particular, could have prompted Scott to attempt it? His high-handed carelessness in cobbling together letters, journal, and direct narrative; his inordinate pleasure in Peter Peebles; his ragged army of rogues and vagabonds, employed indifferently in the furtherance of an overloaded plot—all these may conceal from us the truth that *Redgauntlet* is something more than a romance. It has a theme: the inexorable revolutions of time. That passage of twenty years which condemns any Jacobite plot to futility is set against wider illustrations of the working of time. Scott offers two of these: episodes in the history of his imaginary house of Redgauntlet. The first is the story of Sir Alberic Redgauntlet and the horse-shoe mark—in his worst early German manner.[12]

---

⁹ III. 252–3; Chapter xii.
¹⁰ III. 319; Chapter xxiii.
¹¹ Scott, in his Introduction to the 'Magnum' *Redgauntlet*, acknowledges the discrepancy, at least by implication.
¹² II. 171–7; Chapter viii.

Alberic's misdeed is supposed to determine that every succeeding generation shall find itself on the losing side—but he had formerly brought to life a family of born losers, in the Bertrams of Ellangowan, without the aid of a curse. The second illustration is one of his greatest achievements in the short story, a form he too seldom attempted: a cycle of family history is caught in the magic mirror of Wandering Willie's Tale. Sir Robert Redgauntlet persecuted the 'poor hill folk' in 'the killing time'. Though he survived the Revolution—and this seems to have been an afterthought on Scott's part[13]—retribution followed, not only for succeeding generations of Redgauntlets, but also for those of their humble adherents, the Ste'ensons. (In Scott's estimation, every family has a history.) So it comes about that Hugh Redgauntlet, to all appearance the last of his line, is himself a proscribed fugitive, living precariously among outlaws. This is time's reversal: change Whig for Jacobite, the predicament is the same. Willie, the sole survivor of the Ste'ensons, born blind and orphaned as a child, has grown up in dependence on the house of Redgauntlet, and, with its fall, has become a vagrant fiddler.[14]

Lest I should seem to have made excessive claims for the seriousness of *Redgauntlet*, let me substantiate them by means of a comparison with *Esmond*. The correspondence of design is so close that it can hardly be fortuitous.[15] In each, the adherents of a Stuart Pretender attempt to put back the clock, reverse a former judgement—the success of the Revolution, the ruin of the '45—and fail—as though by a delay of a few hours. But the cause of failure reaches further back. Thackeray's approach to history is deceptively grave and impressive. Behind the conventional, but still useful argument —'They interfered with our women, so we threw them out'— he has traced a pattern of Stuart ingratitude. Disillusion among the supporters of the Pretender is inevitable; but, for

[13] See my examination of the manuscript and proof-sheets: 'Scott and the Art of Revision', in *Notions and Facts*, 1972.

[14] The generations of Redgauntlets and Ste'ensons do not march in step. It may be significant that Scott is liable, throughout, to write son for grandson, and vice versa.

[15] It was noticed at the time, in a review by George Brimley, but the suggestion has not been followed up.

the sake of its impact on the imagination, it must come to a head at a given moment and in a given place. With one reservation, we can claim that Thackeray's contrivance of this culmination—which, like Scott's, is an anticlimax—is a piece of capital workmanship. His management of those last days of Queen Anne's life; his timing of the movements of his characters; his concentration of resources—all these make the happenings at Crackenthorpe's inn seem like a boy's adventure story. Despite Thackeray's caprice and prejudice regarding its historical characters, *Esmond* is solidly built. That reservation, as to its culmination, I have mentioned earlier.[16] Whereas both novelists use the collapse of a conspiracy to resolve their intrigue and give their heroes honourable discharge, Thackeray asks of it no more than this. Inexorable in his depiction of love or loyalty ill bestowed, he is content that its exposure shall release Esmond from servitude both to Beatrix and to the Jacobite dream. I have suggested that the insignificance of Thackeray's Pretender impoverishes Castlewood loyalty to his cause. Scott, no more than Thackeray, would wish that dream realized. Why then is the final impression so different? And why is the difference not altogether in favour of the more accomplished novelist? Both of them know what the imagination of the Common Reader asks of them: that, if anything is to be brought to an end, it shall be by a single, irreversible event. Scott's knowledge (when he is most himself) is so intuitive that it would be safer to say: he proceeds as though he knew. It would, however, be very tedious. I shall therefore say outright: Scott knew that an irreversible event carries overtones of tragedy. Its finality is alien to the comic spirit, whose people may well respond to a popular demand for their return. Scott's Prince will not come again, nor the Jacobite cause revive; but he depicts neither as trivial, and he allows Hugh Redgauntlet to express (in high-flown but not unmeaning terms) the claim that the Jacobites had stood firm for Scottish independence.[17] For Thackeray, successive Stuart claimants could only amass a gambler's pile of debts, a cumulative obligation which must topple into absurdity. I cannot regard Esmond's extravagant

---

[16]   Chapter III, p. 66, above.
[17]   II. 183; Chapter viii.

characterization of the sham duel—that 'immense mark of condescension and repentance for wrong done'—as anything but irony. His later reference to 'the Prince's generous behaviour and their reconciliation' is clearly designed to reassure Rachel Castlewood.[18] No refracted light of irony distorts the end of *Redgauntlet*. With sure judgement, Scott casts back, not to former success but to the ordeal of failure.[19] Time, not folly or mischance, has vanquished the last Pretender. This is what I have called Scott's larger purpose.

Kipling's unforgettable story, 'The Tree of Justice',[20] stands at the end of the series of tales to which it belongs. It is not the latest in time; others carry us down to the Napoleonic wars. Nor does it conclude the argument as to the necessity of Law; that is accomplished in King John's reign. Yet I believe that any reader would be sorry to see it moved; it is in its right place. It may not be the most graceful of the tales; it carries too much meaning. It does not move with that confluence of surprise and a sense of fitness which bears 'The Knights of the Joyous Venture'[21] irresistibly forward. Nevertheless it crowns the work.

There are apparent resemblances to *Redgauntlet*: in both, one who claims, or might claim, the crown returns, too late; in *Redgauntlet*, by twenty years; in 'The Tree of Justice', by 'forty years, less three months and nine days'.[22] In both, loyalty to a fallen dynasty shines like a jewel in the dust. But Kipling does not use the event in the service of a longer, fictitious story. It is contained within itself.

This historical event that never happened is cunningly constructed: Sir Richard Dalyngridge is that most serviceable of narrators, the man who tells all—that is, everything that falls within his observation—because he does not pretend to know all—that is, the significance of everything he observes. Such interpretation as we are vouchsafed belongs to Rahere, and he, like all who perform this function in traditional tales, is both enigmatic and cryptic. Sometimes he speaks in riddles; sometimes he acts out part of a fable. Evidence of identity,

---

[18] Book III, Chapter xiii. [19] III. 319; Chapter xxiii.
[20] *Rewards and Fairies.* [21] *Puck of Pook's Hill.*
[22] This precise date, just short of forty years after the battle of Hastings, and a few weeks before that of Tenchebrai, is given three times, by Sir Richard, by the Pilgrim, and by Rahere.

on which the strange event turns, is disclosed secretly to one of the actors in it; we have his word for it.

Kipling's thought in 'The Tree of Justice' is charged with many and pressing matters: themes which, though they do not conflict, seem to jostle one another for place in so short a story, until the end resolves all differences. There is the welding of Saxon and Norman to make a single nation—an outcome foretold by De Aquila in 'Old Men at Pevensey': ' "In fifty years there will be neither Norman nor Saxon, but all English." ' His enemies' attempt to misrepresent his words merely throws into relief their boldness and sagacity. De Aquila, with his sense of history, is a favourite with his author and an interpreter of the signs of the times, until the story moves into a region between life and death and beyond his apprehension. A kindred issue is discernible in the presentation of Henry I as founder of this nation, in respect of character and other resources: he can rely on the attachment of the men he has made, so long as he has more to give.[23] This theme is sharply focused in the brief exchange at the climax of the story: Rahere has brought the man who was Harold into the presence of the King, flanked by his bishops and barons; Hugh, regardless of self, has acknowledged him, and reproaches Rahere for exposing him in his broken condition.

' "Better have let him die than shame him—and me!" "Shame thee?" said the King. "Would any baron of mine kneel to me if I were witless, discrowned, and alone, and Harold had my throne?" '

There is no answer from the men in attendance on him.

' "No", said Rahere. "I am the sole fool that might do it, Brother, unless"—and he pointed at DeAquila, whom he had only met that day—"yonder tough Norman crab kept me company." '

De Aquila, as has already appeared,[24] stands for feudal loyalty, perhaps a little idealized.

[23] Was Kipling partly indebted to Stubbs's *Constitutional History of England*, or some derivative of that work, for his view of the reign and its significance?
[24] In 'Young Men at the Manor'.

Another development of the historical situation yields Kipling's recurrent theme of the Law—less explicit than it had been in his fable of the framing of Magna Carta, but still intrinsic. It carries none of those metaphysical implications with which he elsewhere charges it, but stands for stability and continuity in government, the King's Peace proclaimed by Henry: ' "I will have it so that though King, son and grandson were all slain in one day, the King's peace should hold over all England! What is a man that his mere death should upheave a people? We must have the Law." '[25] Law signifies security; there is a magnanimity to be looked for at the hands of a sovereign securely estbablished. Time has played its part: the lapse of nearly forty years since the Conquest allows Henry to claim that English troops will fight under him in Normandy. For the sake of this time-interval, Kipling has stretched Harold's life to a length very unlikely in that century, and has masked the improbability by a reference in the opening of the story to a mythical survival and return: '. . . the old rumour waked that Harold the Saxon was alive and would bring them deliverance from us Normans. This has happened every autumn since Senlac fight.' Kipling would get the story of Harold after Hastings from Freeman's *Norman Conquest*,[26] where, though the sources are given as fully as for any historical event, it is dismissed as mythical. Myth takes no account of time; but to the rational mind of the conquerors it is an empty threat:

'Said William of Exeter: "Harold was slain at Santlache fight. All the world knows it."

"I think this man must have forgotten," said Rahere. "Be comforted, Father. Thou wast well slain at Hastings forty years gone, less three months and nine days. Tell the King" '. The King needs no telling. His thoughts reach back to the day when the survival of his own line was in question, and he

---

[25] In 'The Treasure and the Law', however, an essential clause in the Law is extorted from an unjust king by the most downtrodden of his people (*Puck of Pook's Hill*).
[26] (1869), III. 515-17. See C. W. Scott-Giles, 'The Historical Background of some "Puck" Stories', in the *Kipling Journal* (June 1961), pp. 15-21, and Roger Lancelyn Green, *Kipling and the Children* (1965), p. 203.

looks at the man who challenged it. ' "My faith," said Henry after a while, "I think even my Father the Great Duke would pity if he could see him." ' In like manner, General Campbell treats that stately ghost, the vanquished Pretender, with sympathetic courtesy. And so his final departure is not without dignity—and that is something for which we must not look where pity is wanting. When Thackeray dismisses his Pretender as 'a boy, and a French boy',[27] there is no pity for the loser in this dynastic game, and human dignity is cheap.

Kipling does not grudge his fallen king dignity. A little alteration that he makes in the legend may be significant. It had taken Harold to the cloister. Freeman, as historian, recorded this; but, as a stalwart Victorian, he deplored it, and apologized for what he regarded as an unworthy end— even in myth. Kipling, likewise a Victorian, would assent; but as story-teller he was free to substitute another, of his own invention, the life of a poor pilgrim. ('The Miracle of Purun Bhagat', in *The Second Jungle Book* may suggest that it had Indian associations for him.) 'To bide his doom under the open sky' is best, for man—and dormouse. The echo of this theme in the epilogue surely proves that it lies at the heart of the story.

There have been fretful, if not unwarrantable, objections to the intervention of the children in these two books. There can be none to the sentence that brings this tale, and the series,[28] to an end:

' "Dead?" said Una, turning up a white face in the dark.'

It is only after long hesitation that I advance the following illustration of the historical event that never happened— for the consideration of the reader, having been unable to banish it from my own. Here, in bare outline, is the enigma it presents.[29]

'The Book of Sir Thomas More' is a manuscript play by several hands, with additional contributions by yet other

[27] Book III, Chapter xiii. James was 26 and had seen service at Oudenarde and Malplaquet.
[28] 'When those books were finished, they said so themselves'; *Something of Myself*, p. 210.
[29] For a brief list of the authorities on this subject and the development of their argument, see Appendix.

dramatists. The judgement of the highest authorities concurs in attributing one of these additions to Shakespeare. For the purpose of this argument it will be enough to say that I neither could nor would resist the weight of this attribution; that it does not matter who the other dramatists were, though the tenor of the play that they drafted matters very much. I call it a draft, for it appears to have been submitted, as it stood,[30] to 'Edmund Tilney, Master of the Revels, and in that capacity censor of the drama'.[31] Although authority in Elizabethan England did not favour veneration of More,[32] he is presented here as wholly admirable, censure of his opinions being confined to these concluding words:

> A very learned worthy Gentleman
> Seals error with his blood.

But this does not seem to have troubled Tilney. His attention was concentrated on a single episode, that recounting the events of Evil May Day, with More's part in them. According to Halle,[33] feeling in London ran high against the 'aliens', Italian and French, who found that they could ride rough-shod over the citizens, notably merchants and craftsmen, relying on the protection of their ambassadors at Henry VIII's court. Trouble came to a head in the spring of 1517, and broke on the first of May, long remembered as Evil May Day, and thereby a subject for later ballads.[34] The prentices under John Lincoln rioted: they flocked together and released some who had been gaoled for offences against the 'aliens'. More, with other dignitaries, met them and entreated them to go home. When the tumult had subsided, the King sent the earls of Shrewsbury and Surrey to quell it. There were arrests and executions, including not only the ringleader Lincoln, but also 'younglings'. Those who

---

[30] The surviving manuscript is plainly incomplete.

[31] W. W. Greg, Introduction to his edition for the Malone Society, p. x.

[32] R. W. Chambers, *Thomas More* (1935), p. 146, and 'Shakespeare and the Play of "More" ', in *Man's Unconquerable Mind* (1939), p. 212.

[33] Edward Hall or Halle, *Union of the Two Noble and Illustre Families of Lancastre and York*, under the eighth and ninth years of Henry's VIII's reign; the source of this episode.

[34] See below, pp. 127–128.

survived made their submission to the King and were eventually pardoned.

These events form a substantial episode in this loosely episodic play. When it opens, sympathy with the Londoners' grievances, derived from Halle, is indubitable. They err in taking the law into their own hands, but, when persuaded of their error by More, ask him to obtain their pardon from the King—which comes too late to save Lincoln. They accept with stoical patience the likelihood that all must suffer. With one notable exception, the successive incidents keep very close to Halle, even in particulars I have not thought worth mention. Regard for supposed history does not here fall below the level to be expected in a 'history play' of the late sixteenth century. Elsewhere, in the elation of his heart, one of the collaborators identifies the Earl of Surrey who took part in quelling the riot with his son, the poet, and so contrives an opportunity for the introduction of that topic dear to the Elizabethan poet, the low esteem in which poetry is held.[35] More's intercession, though it is the heart of the Evil May Day affair, is distinguished from the rest of this episode in two ways: exceptionally, it does not derive from Halle; neither is it part of the original draft, as that survives in the manuscript. It forms one of the additions to what remains of this play: three pages, known as Addition II (c) in hand D—the hand which palaeographers and literary historians have come to agree in calling Shakespeare's.

Tilney's minor—and presumably initial—marks of censorship throughout the episode fall into two categories: he enjoins the omission of some general references to the dangers of unrest in London, and the substitution of 'Lombards' for 'Frenchmen', and also for 'strangers'. But presently, as though finding these verbal corrections insufficient to allay his disquiet, he writes summarily: 'Leave out the insurrection wholly and the cause thereof, and begin with Sir Thomas More at the Mayor's sessions, being Shrieve of London, upon a mutiny against the Lombards, only by a short report and not otherwise, at your peril.' It has been regarded as a fair

---

[35] *The Book of Sir Thomas More*, ed. W. W. Greg for the Malone Society, pp. 55 and 85. In the latter passage, More reassures Surrey as to the proper standing of his art.

inference that the dramatists concerned did not think it prudent to proceed with the play as it stood, nor worth while to piece together what would remain after Tilney's orders had been carried out.[36]

While Sir Walter Greg saw Tilney's anxiety as the result of endemic unrest stirred by the influx of refugees from the continent, Sir Edmund Chambers particularized: 'The agitation was more or less chronic, but active in 1586, when there were mutterings of another 'Yll May Daye', in 1592-3, and in 1595.'[37] Tilney's injunction to change both Frenchmen and strangers to Lombards would serve to exempt French Huguenots—there had been Frenchmen in Halle, but of a very different sort—and any such Flemish refugees as might be covertly aimed at under the general term.

The problem of the celebrated Addition II (c) is of baffling complexity; and yet, although expert authorities differ as to the order of events and the circumstances in which Shakespeare was invited to provide the crucial scene of More's encounter with the rioters, it may still be possible and useful to spell out a few simple observations. One—perhaps the chief, possibly the sole—aim of the invitation must surely have been to raise More to his proper height: not only is he indisputably the hero of the play, he holds this position principally in virtue of his eloquence; but the homespun, often threadbare, dialogue fails to illustrate this.

If what the original journeyman dramatists required was an illustration of More's 'gentle and persuasive speech', as Surrey calls it,[38] that is certainly what they got—but not only that. Sir Walter Greg says bluntly: 'The writer has no respect for, perhaps no knowledge of, the play on which he is working. His characters are unrecognizable.'[39] (And yet Shakespeare was not unacquainted with Halle.) Not only are the rioters shrunk in stature; their grievances are insignificant. Tilney could not complain of sympathy invoked on their behalf. (When Shakespeare presents characters in humble

---

[36] Greg, Introduction, p. xix. E. K. Chambers does not rule out the possibility of attempted revision: *William Shkespeare, a Study of Facts and Problems* (1930), I. 511-12.

[37] op. cit., p. 511.

[38] p. 14. All references are to Greg's edition.

[39] Introduction, p. xiii.

life as individuals, they are usually sympathetic and can even be, like Cornwall's servant, heroic; but it is evident that he disliked and feared the mob.) So the rioters are diminished, and authority, in the person of the divinely sanctioned sovereign, magnified. What then becomes of those who were the cause of the conflict between them? This is where the strangeness of the story begins.

Unlike the swaggering ruffians of the original draft, they do not appear on the stage; but they are inescapably present to the mind's eye, through More's eloquence:

> Imagine that you see the wretched strangers,
> Their babies at their backs, and their poor luggage,
> Plodding to the coasts and ports for transportation . . .[40]

These are not the protected Italians of Halle's narrative and the play's opening. To the eye of authority, they may well have seemed to resemble far too closely those who had come as refugees from oppression, and, by settling in London, had occasioned the present discontents. How *should* they be regarded?

More's argument moves in a curve—as it were, an arc of which the chord is a reiterated exhortation to his hearers to imagine themselves in a given situation:

> Look, what you do offend you cry upon—
> That is, the peace.

(What the rioters demand threatens to destroy the very protection they enjoy.)

> Had there such fellows lived when you were babes,
> That could have topped the peace as now you would,
> The peace wherein you have till now grown up
> Had been ta'en from you, and the bloody times
> Could not have brought you to the estate of man.

Betts here breaks in with the familiar demand for the removal

---

[40] The three pages occupy pp. 73-8 of Greg's edition, 11. 123-270 of his text. I accept R. W. Chambers's recommendation that quotations should be modernized, as in present-day editions of Shakespeare. See *Man's Unconquerable Mind*, 'Shakespeare and the Play of "More"', p. 213.

of the aliens. Now, with a rapid shift of position, he and his fellows are to imagine themselves spectators of that forlorn procession which their intransigence has set in motion. This is followed by a vision of the rule of lawless might, and that in turn by one of the sovereign as God's vice-regent. Finally, by an abrupt transition, they are to imagine themselves called to account for their turbulence: the King, in his clemency, spares their lives but sentences them to banishment. Thus they are in the very same position as their victims.

> Wither would you go?
> What country by the nature of your error
> Should give you harbour?

So the final vision shows them cowering at the mercy of those who will use them as they propose to use the strangers.

In one respect their case differs from that of their victims. Whereas their part in this remarkable scene has shown them objecting to the 'aliens' for little better reason than that they are foreigners, and are here, they—as More forecasts their banishment—will carry with them the stigma of rebellion. The enmity which they must expect they have brought upon themselves. What Tilney thought of this passage we cannot tell for certain; there is enough gunpowder in the rest of the episode to account for his ban. It is clear only that he wished the story to be fixed in its historical context, and purged of allusions to the power of the London mob. How Shakespeare intended the analogy is a matter of more moment. Was he pleading on behalf of the refugees who had been arriving over the last three decades?[41] Or was his imagination possessed by a wider vision of exile, a threat constantly present to those who lived in an age of religious division? One thing only is certain. He ignored the relatively safe historical context which Tilney required.

That the riot and its consequences remained, in however garbled form, present to the popular imagination is clear from the ballad of 'Ill May-Day'.[42] According to this curious

---

[41] Greg sets the play in the early 1590s.
[42] Alexander Dyce printed the ballad in his edition of *Sir Thomas*

tale, the protected aliens are Spaniards; their assailants are young prentices who turn the licence of May-day revels into a bloody fight; they are taken up in thousands, some hanged forthwith, others brought to trial without hope of mercy. Queen Catherine, moved by pity, pleads for them, though they have assaulted her countrymen. The King astutely grants them conditional pardon, conscripting them for service in his French wars.

Shakespeare alone evokes that image of the eviction for which the rioters have stipulated: a piteous train of refugees. It is of course within the compass of a great dramatist to let even the most reprehensible of his characters speak, and speak well, on his own behalf—witness Shylock. But is there any other instance of a plea quite like this—offered by an intercessor—one, moreover, which goes clean against the grain of tradition? To show Drake helping fugitives from Spanish oppression entails no more than an extension of the character and conduct with which he is credited. To have shown him pleading against the slave-trade would be quite another matter. That More should be remembered as a merciful man, and presented as an advocate for the oppressed, is natural and right. Mr Emrys Jones has pointed out to me the striking analogy between this passage and More's actual plea on be-half of the evicted husbandmen in the First Book of his *Utopia*.[43] But, given the context—that is, the play as it had been conceived and drafted—he must here be supposed to plead for the oppressors—or else for the victims of another and quite different tale of oppression.

What does such a comparison of patently fabulous episodes signify? Nothing, unless this inference be allowed: that, whereas historical fiction differs from history in degree, fictitious history differs in kind. One is embroidery on a given fabric; the other spins and weaves its own fabric, in

---

More for the Shakespeare Society (1844). It is to be found, with in-significant variations, in *A Collection of Old Ballads . . . with Intro-ductions Historical and Critical*, (1725), and in Charles Mackay's *Collection of Songs and Ballads relative to the London Prentices and Trades*, printed for the Percy Society (1841).

[43] Yale edition of the *Complete Works of St. Thomas More* IV (1965), 67.

defiance of the known facts. It therefore poses the question: what impulse of the imagination prompts this singular activity?

Man, as a pattern-making creature, looks for that symmetry in his artifact which he seldom finds in what it represents—his own life and environment. This expectation, in its simpler workings, impels him to find correspondences—a mourning queen for his fallen king, a challenger for his champion. The same impulse prompts a demand that a story shall have a beginning and an end. True, this obligation seems to be just now in abeyance—perhaps because writers are addressing themselves to one another, and are more interested in the process than the product of their work; but the Common Reader finds little satisfaction in the inconclusive story. He may reflect that history—or at least popular history—very often furnishes a beginning: for example, an assassination originating a train of events. There is a more subtle sense of a dire beginning in Kipling's 'Edgehill Fight': not a major battle, nor (we are told) decisive; but the point of no return in that civil war.

> For King or for the Commonweal—
> No matter which they say,
> The first dry rattle of new-drawn steel
> Changes the world to-day!

History seldom offers so clear-cut an end. A decisive battle, yes: Culloden or Waterloo—too big to form part of an imagined narrative, unless that is of the scope of *War and Peace*. Thackeray, with his remarkable insight into the reach of his own art, sets Waterloo within his story but shows us only what led up to it and followed after. The end of a fictitious story may be a smart turn of events—as it were, a well-executed flourish at the foot of the last page; or (in a novel) a convenient disentanglement—the survivors extricated from the knotted situation. Either of these, so far as it gives pleasure, is to be civilly received.

That, however, is by no means the whole matter. If a quite arbitrary verbal distinction may be allowed, for the sake of argument, I shall distinguish between an end and an ending. In narration, an ending is the extinction of a cause, a hope, a dynasty. It makes the climax of *Redgauntlet*, and of 'The Tree of Justice'. In both, though not in *Esmond*, it is an honourable discharge. And in both it speaks from the past to the present. For Scott, the Jacobite dream is over; not because it was unworthy to have been cherished. He borrows from William King the anecdote of the Jacobite expostulating at Stuart obstinacy, but not the sour mood of disillusion.[44] Kipling insists on the narrowness of the margin by which Hastings was won, and the worth of the loyalty which must now be absorbed into another allegiance. Both are concerned with an idea of national unity. What they have further in common is the freedom of fable. They know, and their readers know, and each is aware that the other knows, that what they relate could never have happened. This is the point, I suggest, at which they are joined by Shakespeare. It is on behalf of people at present endangered that he seems to make More plead—as though Portia should turn round at the climax of the trial and plead for the Jews. If this interpretation is valid, then fictitious history liberates the imagination to some purpose.

To this curious tale of writers drawn by imaginative sympathy into the making of fictitious history I venture to add a coda. Whereas the mainspring of those stories was the deliberate employment of anachronism, this little tailpiece is about the story-teller when he takes liberties with time in a different way, and with a different end in view.

On three distinct occasions, Kipling quotes from a Latin hymn of the medieval Church.[45] One—the latest, coming a decade after the conclusion of the Puck stories—is not to my purpose, but must be briefly examined to set off the other two. In 'The Eye of Allah',[46] the few lines quoted serve simply as an historical illustration. The Cantor of the Abbey of St. Illod's is overheard by the Abbot and his guests as he

[44] William King, *Political and Literary Anecdotes of his Own Times*, 2nd edn. (1819), pp. 204–10. King is at pains to justify his own defection.

[45] Kipling would find all three in the collections which awoke interest and prompted translation: for example, J. M. Neale, *Medieval Hymns and Sequences* (1863), and Richard Chenevix Trench, *Sacred Latin Poetry, chiefly Lyrical* (1864).

[46] *Debits and Credits* (1927).

takes his choir through the opening lines of the 'Hora novissima'. The occasion is established in time by the visit of Roger Bacon from Oxford: about the middle of the thirteenth century. The choice of this mid-twelfth-century poem[47] is appropriate enough; its opening topic, the world's benighted state, can be regarded as prelude to the story's theme—a favourite with Kipling: the fate of an untimely invention. Christendom not being ready for the microscope and its revelations, the Abbot foresees censure and persecution by the Church, and is impelled to destroy the model which the wandering artist has brought back from Granada. The poems which precede and follow the story drive this home, the first plainly, the second enigmatically; darkness must give way to light, but not until the appointed time.

The other two passages which carry this freight of Latin verse differ from that plain historical illustration in every respect. Each forms a conclusion to one of the Puck stories, and this generates a peculiar impression, as of that middle state in which a dream expands and brightens before it dissolves. This impression is not shared by the children.

In 'A Centurion of the Thirtieth', Parnesius observes the moment of sunset by prayer to Mithras: 'He rose and stretched his arms westward, with deep, splendid-sounding words. Then Puck began to sing too, in a voice like bells tolling.' Taking the children one by either hand he draws them away, while chanting 'something like this'. What follows is the first stanza and part of the ninth from a thirteenth-century poem on the transience of earthly glory:

> Cur mundus militat sub vana gloria
> Cujus prosperitas est transitoria?
> Tam cito labitur ejus potentia
> Quam vasa figuli quae sunt fragilia.

* * *

[47] A long poem from which English hymns have been carved. It was attributed to Bernard of Cluny; Kipling's Cantor refers familiarly to 'Bernard'.

> Quo Caesar abiit celsus imperio?
> Vel Dives splendidus totus in prandio?
> Dic ubi Tullius . . .[48]

Even as the chanting dies away, the children are borne back, for the time being, to their every-day world. When they encounter Parnesius again, the theme, latent in that first of his three tales, will be developed: the defence of a falling empire. By their devotion, Parnesius and Pertinax will win what we know to be only a respite. But the desperate fighting which will be stayed by the arrival of fresh troops lies hidden in the future: Parnesius has yet to reach the Wall.

Here, then, is a strange confluence of tributaries from diverse catchment areas of history and imagination. A Roman centurion in Christian Britain towards the end of the fourth century prays to Mithras, and the words *that reach us* are those of a thirteenth-century Franciscan friar, while the voice is Puck's. Our perplexity may be lessened if we allow the surmise that Kipling was using Mithraism as an emblem. As such it appears in the last of the three Roman-British stories,[49] where he seems to regard it as he regarded Freemasonry: a creed ('faith and works' sustained by ritual) transcending all human divisions but one, that between men and women. ' "I knew" ', Parnesius says when he recognizes a 'brother' in Amal, ' "that those who worship Mithras are many and of all races." '[50] It is boundaries not only of place that are here transcended, but of time also—nine whole centuries of it. Indeed, we may add six more, if we come to believe that Kipling was writing in the mood of his own 'Recessional':[51]

[48] *Oxford Book of Mediaeval Latin Verse*, ed. F. J. E. Raby (1959), no. 284; (not in original edition). Anonymous poem of the thirteenth century, sometimes ascribed to Jacopone da Todi; see F. J. E. Raby, *A History of Christian Latin Poetry* (1927), p. 435.

[49] 'The Winged Hats', *Puck of Pook's Hill.*

[50] This is a recurring idea. In the verse, a development of it may be divined in 'Banquet Night' (' "Once in so often", King Solomon said'), where the bond is that of craftsmanship.

[51] See A. W. Rutherford 'Officers and Gentlemen', in his collection, *Kipling's Mind and Art* (1936), p. 195. He presses the comparison—perhaps too far—in a stimulating essay.

> Lo, all our pomp of yesterday
> Is one with Nineveh and Tyre!

Here is not that nice manipulation of time that we are used to calling anachronism.

The introduction of a Latin hymn into 'The Conversion of St. Wilfrid'[52] is, in a different way, quite as curious: the *'Dies Irae'*[53] heard (in a nineteenth-century musical setting) by an Anglo-Saxon 'Archbishop' of the seventh century. Again, the context is the end of a dream, which swells and fades as the children emerge from it. At home in their parish church, they have been listening to 'the Lady who practises the organ', and to St. Wilfrid's recollections, pieced out by Puck, of an episode in his arduous and eventful life.[54] As the tale draws to an end, 'the Lady' finishes her practice and, to please the children, plays the accompaniment to a romantic setting of the *'Dies Irae'*. From the deepening shadows of the church come the words, distinctly uttered, of the first, third, and ninth stanzas of the requiem. They cannot be audible to 'the Lady', who continues her playing, undistracted by the magic. To the children they appear to be part of that mysterious Latin which is found in churches, where it is harmless.[55] But they are heard by the Saint: ' "Oh, what a marvel of a voice!" said the Archbishop'—and by Puck. We may say, particularly by Puck, since he joins in.

What these two passages have in common, besides and beyond their visionary atmosphere and the bold treatment of time, is Puck's peculiar function in them. Kipling's own definition of the scope and aim of his Puck books is well known: they were to speak first to children, but also to grown people, who would find still further meaning in them. This dictated the method, complex and assiduous, but a labour of love. 'It was glorious fun.'[56] There I find an

---

[52] *Rewards and Fairies.*
[53] *Oxford Book of Mediaeval Latin Verse*, no. 259, by Thomas of Celano, thirteenth century.
[54] The troubles of the time, and the vicissitudes of the Saint's career, must be held to account for this 'Prince of the Church' holding a cure of souls on a barren stretch of half-pagan coast. He was *Bishop* of York.
[55] See p. 158, below.
[56] *Something of Myself*, pp. 190–1.

intimation of yet another audience: surely he was writing to please himself, and to gain that reassuring sense of continuity he needed. In the first book, a theme is proffered and developed. At the end of the last story, Puck spells it out: ' "Weland gave the Sword! The Sword gave the Treasure, and the Treasure gave the Law. It's as natural as an oak growing." '[57] But this is superficial compared with the habitual and instinctive thinking in the verse: notably, 'Cities and Thrones and Powers'. Helplessly perishable, we must believe in some sort of continuance. ('Thou turnest man to destruction: again thou sayest, Come again, ye children of men.')

Of this deper meaning, Puck is not so much the spokesman as the symbol. True, the part he plays in these two books is variable. He is throughout the kindly, serviceable mediator between the children and their visitants—only now and then officious. He can, however, be charged with a meaning bigger than any in his explicit utterances—indeed, he is most revealing when least didactic. Like Hobden in one respect, he testifies to a capacity for survival. But Hobden survives in virtue of historical fact:

> His dead are in the churchyard,
>   thirty generations laid.
> Their names were old in history
>   when Domesday book was made.[58]

Puck's longevity is proper to myth. It is often the poets who throw the clearest light on one another, simply by giving a seemingly fortuitous opportunity for comparison. In one of his poems, Edward Thomas evokes the image of an old countryman whose face haunted him. The uncertain and contradictory accounts he gets in neighbouring villages presently give place to the authority of myth.

> Do you believe Jack dead before his hour?

He, under many names,

---

[57] 'The Treasure and the Law'. Dan's objections are never answered, nor Una's hope of an explanation fulfilled.
[58] 'The Land' ('When Julius Fabricius, Sub-Prefect of the Weald').

Although he was seen dying at Waterloo,
Hastings, Agincourt, and Sedgemoor too,—
Lives yet.[59]

There is something of Puck here; but for the full, rounded impression of timelessness, of a world in which time is in abeyance, Kipling needed that voice chanting passages from Latin hymns.

[59] 'Lob', in *Collected Poems* by Edward Thomas (1974).

Chapter VI
The Problem of Language

The problem of language may be initially framed as a question: how should the characters in a tale speak, if we are to suppose that they lived in another age than ours, and how should the narrator write, if we are to suppose him their contemporary? Scott makes the answer appear simple. He claims that Horace Walpole, in *The Castle of Otranto*, 'adheres to the sustained tone of chivalry which marks the period of the action. This is not attained by patching his narrative or dialogue with glossarial terms, or antique phraseology, but by taking care to exclude all that can awaken modern associations.'[1] This proposition is open to challenge on two counts. A language formed on such a negative prescription would be *pithless*. Moreover, it is certainly not the language Horace Walpole here employs. Not only do his thirteenth-century characters quote Shakespeare;[2] their speech is throughout that of the eighteenth-century stage, in its higher, more unsteady flights. This is odd, but not peculiar. In an age when to taunt a speaker with talking from 'play-books' was tantamount to an accusation of rant and fustian,[3] the old and ailing stage still dominated the young and lusty novel, where either aimed above comedy. Contemporary illustrations tell their own tale. There is a family resemblance between those in *The Castle of Otranto* and in Sir Thomas Hanmer's Shakespeare:[4] the persons in both wear what may be described as masquerade dress, richer and more fanciful than that of everyday life in the eighteenth century, but belonging to no other age.

---

[1] *Life of Walpole*, in *Miscellaneous Prose Works* (1827), III. 384–5.

[2] Pointed out by W. S. Lewis in the Introduction to his edition (1964), p. xix.

[3] *Rob Roy*, II. 19; Chapter xvii.

[4] 1744. Sir Thomas, as David Nichol Smith remarks, edited Shakespeare 'by the light of his own taste' (*Shakespeare in the Eighteenth Century* (1928), p. 43).

'To avoid all that can awaken modern associations'—this may sound simple and even practicable, but the history of literary forgery shows it to be impossible. Imposture which passes muster in its own day betrays itself to the ear of any succeeding generation not so much by overt allusions as by tacit assumptions. In dialogue, this may mean a mere turn of phrase, hardly more than the equivalent of a tone of voice. Now that our own language is studied more systematically than hitherto, the writer is better equipped for deception— but so are his readers, for detection. Besides, a language constructed solely on principles of avoidance can be very dull.

That this recommendation should come from Scott, who had himself discovered a better way, is explicable on two counts: he was writing about a story set in medieval Italy, and his own recent[5] novels had been set almost as far off, alike in time and place. None of them afforded opportunity for the procedure he had advocated in his Advertisement to *The Antiquary*, and had put to good use, there and in *Guy Mannering*. He has, he explains, chosen his principal characters from those 'classes' most tenacious of past ways, finding among them readiness to feel and express passion. Here, a polite bow to Wordsworth. This, he continues, is notably true of the Scottish peasantry. 'The antique force and simplicity of their language often tinctured with the oriental eloquence of Scripture, in the mouths of those of an elevated understanding, gives pathos to their grief, and dignity to their resentment.' Wordsworth, however, had not represented his countrymen as speaking any dialect. Nor had anything been said, in the original Advertisement to the *Lyrical Ballads*, about a peculiar attachment to past ways on the part of characters in the narrative poems. References to 'our elder writers', 'the elder poets', denote the literary tradition to which the two authors adhere.[6]

That the use of one or another variant of his native tongue for dialogue in these novels was an innovation on Scott's

[5] Walpole', in *The Lives of the Novelists*, was 'completed by the end of February 1823'. See Grierson, *Sir Walter Scott*, p. 205 n.

[6] It seems probable that Scott is referring to the Advertisement of 1798; and what the Preface of 1800 adds has no bearing on this idea of antiquity.

part is suggested by Croker's acrimonious conclusion to an otherwise favourable review of *The Antiquary*: if the glossary which is 'almost indispensable to the understanding of nine-tenths of the work', had been placed at the beginning, he would not have had to labour unaided 'through the dark dialect of Anglified Erse'.[7] A passing reference in the next (July) number of the *Quarterly* looks like a remonstrance: in a review of numerous travel books, a distinction is drawn between merely vulgar speech and a provincial dialect, which is 'only a different and antiquated form' of our language—notably as it has been used by 'men of genius', such as Burns, and Scott in *The Antiquary*.[8]

Here I am obliged to insert an apology and explanation. No philologist, I am at a loss for terms. *Dialect* will not do for the range of speech patterns comprised in Lowland Scots. Neither will *language*, which would set it on the same footing, as to distinctness, with Gaelic. *Tongue*, even as I wrote it, sounded too poetic. I understand that 'language variety' is the correct designation. But it will not serve my purpose when I want to say simply that such and such a character is to be *heard* speaking Scots, whatever the means taken to indicate this; or that his way of speaking makes such and such a contribution to the total impression. (Such speakers are to be regarded rather as instruments in an orchestra than witnesses to philological fact.) I propose therefore to use the word *idiom*, except where the context justifies another of these various terms.

The question now arises: does Scott's use of his native idiom carry reverberations of the past—today, everywhere? In facing this question, we are concerned first with impression, and only secondarily with the means by which it is conveyed. The very symbols, the notation, will often turn out to be the product of mere convention. Scott himself is on such easy terms with them that he sometimes leaves it to Ballantyne to insert the conventional spelling.[9] Nevertheless, the impres-

---

[7] *Quarterly* for April 1816, xv, 139. For the attribution to Croker, see Corson's *Bibliography*, item 1475.

[8] p. 560.

[9] 'Ballantyne may have been responsible for observing the convention as to Scottish spellings for certain common words. Scott undoubtedly *heard* the words in his own tongue, but he seldom troubled

sion holds: for the imaginative reader, those novels of Scott and Stevenson which are set in eighteenth-century Scotland—that is, within reach of hearsay-memory for their authors—achieve their sense of the past largely by means of the language given to their characters.

One indication of this—as insistent as a weather-sign—is the way in which both employ Scottish idiom to differentiate the generations. Though characters in humble life use it habitually, if with slight variations, those who, if they were English, would all speak much alike may differ according to their age. *Weir of Hermiston* affords an illustration. Adam Weir, spokesman for the past, uses the Scots idiom deliberately, ostentatiously. In Glenkindie's speech, it may be adopted or exaggerated to sharpen provocation. But in neither of these old and eminent men is it socially eccentric. In Kirstie it is natural, and necessary: in no other tongue could she evoke that older world of heroic violence in which the Elliotts still dwell, and into which Archie will be drawn. The absence of Scoticisms from his habitual speech does not simply assign him to the younger generation; it has not the callow smartness of Frank Innes's style. Nor is Stevenson here conforming with Scott's practice and seeming expectation that the hero shall speak English, no matter in what household he has been reared. (It is no wonder that Henry Morton is nearly shot by his own side.) It is true that Archie Weir's speech, as it confronts us on the printed page, alienates him strangely from both father and mother; but we have been shown enough of his childhood and youth to surmise that his idiom may be the result of fastidious refinement, in conscious antagonism to his father, and sympathy with the man he would have chosen for father, Lord Glenalmond. It would, however, be a mistake to give either of these two, in reading aloud, an English *intonation*. Moreover, in his passionate appeal to young Kirstie for understanding, Archie himself slips into a phrase that no English speaker would use: ' "Kirstie", he cried, "O

---

to mark the distinction in the first draft. His revision tends in this direction, but fitfully.' See my essay on Scott's revision of Wandering Willie's Tale, in *Notions and Facts*, p. 221. Mrs Tillotson points out that his injunction to Ballantyne to 'ready this'—not, as I supposed, read this (p. 219)—was a printing-house term, allowing him some discretion.

Kirstie woman!" '[10] She, for her part, habitually uses the idiom of her family, a little softened; but, when she wishes to stand on her dignity, she can *mince*.

In this context, a brief comparison with *Castle Rackrent* may be useful. Maria Edgeworth tells her story in the idiom, steadly sustained, of its imagined chronicler, Thady M'Quirk, steward to past generations of Rackrents. She acknowledges that she has made him older than his original, John Langan,[11] and she shows him as a forlorn ghost in the present. For its latest editor, this promotes *Castle Rackrent* to the position of earliest historical novel.[12] Mrs Butler, however, draws another inference: she shows the importance to the reforming Edgeworths, as they looked forward to the imminent Union, of fixing the story and its narrator in a past on which Ireland had shut the door,[13] and she finds evidence of political expediency in Maria's emphatic assurance that there are no such people as the Rackrents and their steward in the Ireland of her day.[14] For me, Mrs Butler's argument and authority prevail. The Glossary, as she points out, was an anxious afterthought: no mere word-list, like that in *The Antiquary*, but an amplification of the original footnotes, designed to further this aim of confining Thady and his subject to the irrecoverable past. What matters, however, is the concurrence of these two interpreters on the idea of *time past*, and Thady as its chronicler in its own idiom. This is indubitable. 'The Editor' —Maria herself—'had it once in contemplation to translate the language of Thady into plain English; but Thady's idiom is incapable of translation, and besides, the authenticity of his story would have been more exposed to doubt if it were not told in his own characteristic manner!'[15]

Scott's practice is more various. He has a wider field to till, and he raises a flourishing crop, together with the usual

[10] Chapter ix.
[11] Marilyn Butler, *Maria Edgeworth* (1972), p. 240, quoting from a letter.
[12] George Watson, Introduction, in the Oxford English Novelists edition (1964), p. viii.
[13] op. cit., p. 355.
[14] ' . . . the race of the Rackrents has long since been extinct in Ireland', Preface (in Oxford edition, p. 5); frequently reiterated.
[15] ibid., p. 4.

flamboyant weeds. He uses his native idiom resourcefully. The first purpose which, like any manner of speech, it must serve is to define and distinguish character; but, his conception of character being generic, what his fully developed characters have to say and their way of saying it will carry overtones of time and place. Jeanie Deans is individual in the sense that she is unique. No one, not Scott himself, could ever make such another. At the same time, she is representative of a particular national strain and of the faith and opinions in which, at a given point in the history of her nation, she was reared. And (until that unhappy fourth volume) no word, phrase, or cadence is out of keeping with this context.

It must be admitted that Scott, with Stevenson in his train, enjoyed an advantage denied to any English novelist who should attempt to establish his tale in a past time and a particular place by means of an English dialect. Throughout the whole island it was possible to claim for Scots a literary, even a poetic, standing. This, I believe, had something to do with the regard in which the northern ballad was held. Even from the day when 'Chevy Chase'—or was it 'The Battle of Otterbourne'?—so stirred Sidney's heart,[16] on through Addison's testimony of approval,[17] the eighteenth-century collections and nineteenth-century imitations, the ballad has commanded a distinctive eminence, and, unless qualified—for example, by a reference to Robin Hood—has been taken to mean border ballad. Murmur the single word in the ear of any poetically literate hearer, and you will get some such meditative response as this: 'Oh yes, "The Wife of Usher's Well", or "Sir Patrick Spens", or "The Douglas Tragedy" ', or this or that, according to inclination. The train of association will probably run: verse tale, of a distant past, sombre in tone, set in the north and delivered in the Scottish tongue. It has been strengthened by literary practice: in the eighteenth century, by an extension of the tradition—sequels rather than counterfeits, and the best of these are in Scots; in the nineteenth, by conscious

---

[16] 'Apology for Poetry' (in *Elizabethan Critical Essays*, ed. Gregory Smith (1904), I. 178).
[17] *Spectator*, numbers 70 and 74. 'Chevy Chase' was known to Addison in a debased version. See D. F. Bond's edition of *The Spectator* (1965), I. 298, n. 1.

imitation, and these pretenders attempt the same idiom. Thus there is nothing forbiddingly strange in the speech of Edie Ochiltree or Meg Merrilies; yet it stretches the imagination, notably in a particular direction. We apprehend them not merely as denizens of an earlier world than that in which Scott himself lived and wrote, but also as men and women able to look further back still. They give depth in time, as pictorial perspective gives depth in space; and they give this to the whole novel. They may be likened to rivers which keep their identity, and their (usually archaic) names, no matter what diverse regions they irrigate. They are not like those characters who symbolize the secret, withdrawn life of the mountains.

All this, it may be said—the tradition and the response it draws from us—are merely Scott's birthright—though it would be a churlish spirit who should therefore deny him credit for a privilege of which he makes such good use. He deploys his linguistic resources with deliberate art. This is how Chrystal Croftangry, himself a Scot, analyses the speech of Mrs Bethune Balliol: 'It was Scottish, decidedly Scottish, often containing phrases and words little used in the present day.' And this distinction is particularized: 'It seemed to be the Scottish as spoken by the ancient court of Scotland, to which no idea of vulgarity could be attached; and the lively manner and gestures with which it was accompanied, were so completely in accord with the sound of the voice and the manner of talking, that I cannot assign them a different origin.'[18] Unfortunately, the tales which she is said to have told so well are consigned in writing at her death to Croftangry —a favourite device of Scott's—and told in his habitual narrative style. (How the real author comes to terms with their dialogue is another matter.)

One reason for this, I suggest, is that Scott himself could not command an accepted notation—that is, a system of spelling-conventions which would proclaim, from the printed page, how such speech as this should be heard, in the *mind's ear*; it was outside the range of customary, and therefore accepted, spelling-devices. To this problem of notation I

---

[18] *I Canongate*, p. 132; Chapter vi.

must presently return. Meanwhile, it is important to notice that not only will the Scots spoken in the cottage as a matter of course vary from one district to another; that spoken, notably by the older characters, in the great house has its variations, and fluctuations: they do not all speak alike, nor does any one of them speak always in the same way. Lady Margaret Bellenden, for example, uses a more markedly Scottish idiom when she is disputing with Mause Headrigg than when she is speaking with her brother-in-law; while, for his part, Miles Bellenden, true type of the travelled Scot, keeps a few native idioms in reserve for moments when he is moved beyond his usual urbanity. ' "It's a hard thing to hear a hamely Scotch tongue cry quarter and be obliged to cut him down . . ." '[19]

There is another idiosyncrasy of speech, somewhere between language and thought, which Scott uses to define character. Neither so simple, nor (unless it is overworked) so tedious as the catch-phrase, the habit of reference to an abiding preoccupation gives a broad stroke of characterization. Such a habit may amount to obsession, as when the untiring litigant comes to believe himself a lawyer. It may mean no more than a tendency to refer every current topic to the measure of the speaker's own craft or calling: we are not allowed to forget that Nicol Jarvie is a linen-merchant and magistrate. But the most frequent preoccupation of Scott's older characters is with some phase of past history. This is not the kind of historical insight with which Kipling endows De Aquila, a perspective of past, present, and future which he shares with his author. It is more like a private vista into the past. Thus, when Lady Margaret Bellenden confronts Mause Headrigg with arguments from history, Mause seems to counter with Biblical references; but, taking into account the Covenanters' preoccupation with the historical books of the Old Testament and their inclination to regard Israelite history as an emblematical foreshadowing of their own, the difference is not so great. Each appears to be looking along a sort of smugglers' road, sunk deep and heavily overshadowed.

The elaborately archaic style of Scott's Covenanters,

[19]   *Old Mortality*, II. 279; Chapter xi.

marking their historical obsession, was diligently gathered from their memoirs; but his success in reproducing these very sources denies Scott the use of a distinctly Scottish vocabulary in their talk. Even the spelling is normal. How then are we supposed to *hear* this 'language variety' when they carry on the dialogue? What means were available for making the printed page *speak*? When he is not hampered by his fidelity to written sources, Scott has at his disposal certain established conventions.

Set aside, for the present, such words as may be called, in Scott's dismissive phrase, 'glossarial terms', and there remain many that are common to English and Scots, but which we are meant to hear with a difference—one customarily indicated by a conventional divergence of spelling. The philologist will condem this convention as wanting phonetic authenticity.[20] From the Common Reader there is diversity of response. At one end of the scale are those who recognize in these written symbols a compulsion to hear—and, if they are reading aloud, to utter—these words as they sound in their own native tongue. Then come the ordinary English readers, whose mind's ear can approximate at least to the rhythm if not to the quality of the sounds in phrase or sentence. At the tail follow those of such southerly inclination that, like Croker, they can discern nothing on the page but a tiresome eccentricity of spelling.These, I maintain, might be in the majority, if it were not for the double spell of the ballads and Scott's own achievement, in his ballads and ballad-snatches and memorable passages of prose dialogue. When Ratcliffe retorts to Madge's accusation of double-dealing, ' "I never shed blood" ', she thrusts home: ' "But ye hae sauld it, Ratton—ye hae sauld blood mony a time. Folk kill wi' the tongue as weel as wi' the hand . . ." '.[21] Here is nothing strange either in words or word-order, but what reader of ordinary linguistic sensibility would call out for normal spelling?

As for the hard words which prompted even Lady Louisa Stuart to plead for a glossary to *Old Mortality* like that in

---

[20] For the rise of interest in systems of phonetic spelling and Sir James Murray's dissatisfaction with current devices, see K. M. Elizabeth Murray, *Caught in the Web of Words* (1977), pp. 74–6, and *passim*.

[21] *Heart of Midlothian*, II. 120; Chapter xvii.

The Antiquary,[22] they are, for the most part, found among the broadly comic passages; our understanding of the tenor of the story, its deeper currents, seldom depends on familiarity with them.

I have tried to approach by way of argument and illustration the position which G. M. Trevelyan authoritatively maintains: 'The Scots of the later Eighteenth Century were Sir Walter's own folk, and their shrewd, poetic, forceful talk was his own mother tongue. Their character and their conversation could be transplanted, with historical likelihood enough, a century and a half back.'[23]

Every candid reader, however, must be disconcerted by the transition from such dialogue to Scott's habitual narrative style. It is a very abrupt change to the present—his present day; and it is too often a change for the worse. This does not apply to a story whose dialogue and narrative are framed in the same idiom—such as Wandering Willie's Tale, or Stevenson's spirited imitation of it, The Tale of Tod Lapraik.[24] Here the spell holds; and it is almost as strong in those other tales woven into the fabric of *Redgauntlet*, the recollections of Maxwell of Summertrees and Nanty Ewart.

All these are told supposedly by word of mouth, and there is a constant reminder of the narrator's manner of speech in the spelling. Stevenson is confronted by a different problem when he commits his story-teller to a written record, and that by a more literate chronicler than Thady M'Quirk. He liked first-person narrative, and was ready, as usual, with a theory to support his preference.[25] The novel-reader was familiar with the tradition of a story told by the titular hero, and ready to accept its conventions, but Mackellar asked

[22] Letter to Scott, 5 Dec. 1816; (*Sir Walter Scott's Letters*, ed. David Douglas (1894), I. 394).

[23] *An Autobiography and Other Essays* (1949), pp. 202-3. See also David Daiches, '*Redgauntlet*', in *From Jane Austen to Joseph Conrad, Essays Collected in Memory of J. T. Hillhouse* (1958), p. 57: Wandering Willie's Tale is told in 'late eighteenth-century Scots'.

[24] In *Catriona*, part of Chaper xi. Is his use of the name Lapraik to be understood as an avowal of indebtedness? Laurie Lapraik is a character in Scott's tale.

[25] 'Note to "The Master of Ballantrae"', Vailima edition, XXVI. 479. 'He began theorising—as he does about everything under the sun'; (*Memories of Vailima*, p. 51).

something more. Not only was he set at an angle to the Durie chronicle, no kin to the protagonists but tied to their fortunes by loyalty. His narrative is set at a distance from the events which determine its course. Stevenson originally designed to widen this interval: he invented a framework—Mackellar's papers were to be opened and read only after the lapse of fifty years. He presently relinquished this, as too much like Scott—and so it is, only better—but finally intended to restore it.[26] The anecdote is worth recovering for its own sake, but the distance is already there. Here Mackellar tells of the departure to North America and (as he hopes) to safety of the family he serves, and of his own reaction:

I never knew before the greatness of that vault of night in which we two poor serving-men—the one old, and the one elderly—stood for the first time deserted . . . It seemed that we who remained at home were the true exiles, and that Durrisdeer and Solwayside, and all that made my country native, its air good to me, and its language welcome, had gone forth and was far over the sea with my old masters.

He paces to and fro, through the night.

Day came upon the inland mountain-tops, and the fowls began to cry, and the smoke of homesteads to arise in the brown bosom of the moors, before I turned my face homeward, and went down the path to where the roof of Durrisdeer shone in the morning by the sea.[27]

There speaks out of the past the voice of an elderly Scotsman as he looks back to a time when, already ageing, he saw his own past ebbing, even as that of his master had ebbed ever since the '45.

Mackellar ceased to please Stevenson at the end; but, by

[26] See *Letters to Baxter*. On 2 January 1888 he writes from Lake Saranac—date and place editorial—asking C.B. to collaborate in the pretence. He is to suppose that he has succeeded to the practice and archives of the firm of lawyers in whose hands Mackellar had placed his record: 'the Duries were extinct; and last year, in an old green box, you found these papers . . .' (p. 184). About 18 May 1894 (date editorial) he wrote from Samoa to say that he had already written this preface, had 'then condemned the idea as being a little too like Scott, I suppose', but now wishes it to be included in the projected Edinburgh edition (p. 355).

[27] Chapter ix.

that time he felt an unappeasable hunger to be done with the work. Moreover, both the 'Genesis' and the 'Note' perplex: he defends the Chevalier Burke. It is neither prudent nor polite to *know better than* your author; but Burke seems to me a cheap expedient, and dear at the price. As to Mackellar, he surely serves the purpose I have intimated: he establishes the story in eighteenth-century Scotland.[28] It might be objected to the illustration I have given that it stands at a moment of crisis in the speaker's life; but is it a mere literary convention that allows characters to speak more deeply out of themselves at such moments than we usually do? Even so, the reader's pulse will answer to this heightened language so long as it is poetry and not fustian.

To sum up, so far: Scott and Stevenson use dialogue in a variety of ways, at their best subtle and unobtrusive, to establish their story in a Scotland earlier than their own, often looking back to one which is older still. To this I would add a surmise: these intimations of a manner of speech come most persuasively from one who can on occasion speak the language himself. The thieves' cant which Jeanie Deans overhears may, for all I know, be correctly reproduced; but it seems to want the authenticity of the idiom spoken, with due variations, by her family and the Butlers. This may prove true of another of Scott's *collection* of idioms.

Preoccupied as he was with the idea of the Highlander living in a separate world, alienated from the present, Scott had to come to terms with Gaelic-speaking characters, the representation of their idiom in English or Scots, and of their language when they are speaking in their own tongue. To the first of these he brought no more than a few words and phrases of Gaelic, together with an attentive ear for the linguistic predicament of those who must think in one language but speak in another. Reflecting on the parting speech of Helen MacGregor, Frank Osbaldiston is made to say:

[28] For Stevenson's theories about first-person narration, see 'Genesis of "The Master of Ballantrae" '; likewise for his defence of Burke in this part. For his dissatisfaction with Mackellar, see 'Note to "The Master of Ballantrae" ', with the further pages printed in E. N. Caldwell, *Last Witness*, pp. 117–19. For his weariness and dissatisfaction with the novel, see, e.g., his letter to Colvin, *Letters*, Colvin, IV. 108; from Vailima, 15 Sept. [1892].

There was a strong provincial accentuation, but, otherwise, the language rendered by Helen MacGregor, out of the native and poetical Gaelic, into English, which she had acquired as we do learned tongues, but had probably never heard applied to the mean purposes of ordinary life, was graceful, flowing, and declamatory. Her husband, who had in his time played many parts, used a much less elevated and emphatic dialect,— but even *his* language rose in purity of expression, when the affairs which he discussed were of an agitating and important nature; and it appears to me in his case, and in that of some other Highlanders whom I have known, that, when familiar and facetious, they used the Lowland Scottish dialect,—when serious and impassioned, their thoughts arranged themselves in the idiom of their native language; and in the latter case, as they uttered the corresponding ideas in English, the expressions sounded wild, elevated, and poetical. In fact, the language of passion is almost always pure as well as vehement, and it is no uncommon thing to hear a Scotchman, when overwhelmed by a countryman with a tone of bitter and fluent upbraiding, reply by way of taunt to his adversary, 'You have gotten to your English.'[29]

Diligently followed throughout its meanderings, this passage accounts for Scott's practice so long as his Highlanders are not using their own tongue. Volume One of the First Series of *Chronicles of the Canongate*, a late, uneven work and (perhaps for that reason) unduly neglected, illustrates his approach to both branches of this problem. Janet MacEvoy's part in the first few chapters, the frame-story, develops a new vein of gentle comedy in Scott's art. Using his favourite device of simple contrast, he sets her over against Christie Steele, the implacably righteous Lowlander, who rejects Chrystal Croftangry—not without reason: she has been his mother's maid, and he has been a bad son. Janet, refugee from the dispeopled Highland glens, has eked out a scanty livelihood by letting lodgings in the Canongate where Croftangry formerly sought a debtor's sanctuary. When he returns, prosperous but disheartened, she becomes his housekeeper, and, in compliance with tradition, occasional literary confidante. Owing him nothing but the odd change from a former payment, she

[29] *Rob Roy*, II. 244-5; Chapter xxxv. It is of course Scott himself speaking.

devotes to him a clanswoman's loyalty. Compared with the ready, and mordant, tongue of Christie Steele, hers is the peculiar idiom of the immigrant, who, thinking in one language, speaks in another—fluent enough, but distinguished from the native citizens of Edinburgh by such peculiarities as spelling can indicate, and a few turns of phrase. She has, for example, brought with her from the Gaelic the habit of speaking of herself in the third person. Any sense of impeded utterance, however, is swept away in a flood of eloquence when she speaks of the remembered, or fabled past, of Highland life as she recalls it. Now ' "the glen is desolate, and the braw snoods and bonnets are gane, and the Saxon's house stands dull and lonely, like the single bare-breasted rock that the falcon builds on—the falcon that drives the heath-bird frae the glen" '. Janet, Croftangry comments, 'like many Highlanders, was full of imagination; and, when melancholy themes came upon her, expressed herself almost poetically, owing to the genius of the Celtic language in which she thought, and in which, doubtless, she would have spoken, had I understood Gaelic'.[30]

In the two tales which follow, and complete this volume in the first edition,[31] Scott returns to an old theme, with a difference. (Is it significant that Janet, called in to test by her sensibility the probable response of the reader, weeps only when a Cameron is killed?) In *Waverley*, that ancient world of the Highlander had died with Evan Dhu, and Scott spoke its obituary in the Postcript. Here, he sees it as holding one or another of its denizens in a relentless grip, forbidding them to recognize it as a lost Atlantis, and to make terms with the present. Of these two, 'The Highland Widow' and 'The Two Drovers', the first is the more intrinsically tragic: the victim is destroyed by his mother, to whom he is all the world. In the second, destruction comes from mischance and the malice of strangers. Nevertheless, it is by far the more powerful. What the other gains by its concentration within a close family relationship, it loses by an error of judgement in the choice and use of language.

---

[30] p. 95; Chapter v.
[31] Scott yielded to Ballantyne's remonstrance in 1827 and threw out two tales and an anecdote, but restored them in the 'Magnum'. See *Journal*, p. 421 (31 Jan. 1828).

In 'The Highland Widow', Elspat MacTavish, Volumnia to a younger and more innocent Coriolanus,[32] is not merely a Highlander who thinks in Gaelic and would prefer to speak it; she is to be imagined as speaking it throughout. This opens before the story-teller a choice of ways: either he must himself think in that other language and translate thought into English—the language by which he communicates with his readers; or he must find—either make or borrow—an idiom which will serve his purpose. Scott had not—and did not claim—enough Gaelic for the first. He was therefore committed to an invented idiom.

There is something odd, even paradoxical, in such a situation. Whereas the translator wishes you to forget the linguistic difference between his original and the version he offers you, the story-teller whose characters are supposedly using a foreign tongue means you to remember this. Like the translator, he seeks an equivalent, but one with insistent overtones. Your sense of strangeness must be, though not oppressive, constant. To invent an idiom asks for inclination and aptitude of a peculiar kind. It may, but need not, require philological nor even literary cunning. It is sometimes found in a close-knit family of children; but, since what they invent is, like the 'little language' of lovers, a secret, they cannot be cited as witnesses, though echoes of their play may sometimes be heard among those who write *for* them. Scott was a bold and usually plausible collector of idioms, but not an inventor. He was therefore content to borrow a formula for the speech of Elspat Mac-Tavish. This is a pity, for, not only is she the most active character in the story; she is the principal speaker. She lures, tricks and bemuses her son into the fatal situation where he will kill a fellow-soldier and pay with his life; and, except for the opiate drink, she effects all this with words—and still has words to spare for her amazement at the outcome of her design. Although Scott was sceptical of Macpherson's

[32] The analogy is signalized by the three lines chosen to head Chapter xii:

> But for your son, believe it—oh, believe it—
> Most dangerously you have with him prevailed,
> If not most mortal to him.

larger pretensions,[33] he seems content to poach on his preserves of language. Elspat has only two moods, exhortation and execration. That 'Ossianic' dialect does nothing to relieve the monotony of their unvaried pitch. Elaborately figurative, it draws its images from a narrow range of objects. The eagle, feebly supported by the raven, has to do duty for the fowls of the air; the adder and wolf for the rest of creation. This artifice may link the speaker with a fabulous past—but at a ruinous cost. Scott had surely been right in doubting whether the tale would 'endure much expansion'; wrong, when he came to think it written his 'bettermost manner'.[34]

'The Two Drovers' follows hesitantly on this tale.[35] At the outset, Scott develops yet again his former apology: this time Croftangry tells Janet what Mrs Bethune Balliol had formerly told him, that the Highlands are a worked-out mine. He was presently to acknowledge that both stories had seized his imagination a long while ago—that is, before his imitators followed him into that territory: the first derived from Mrs Murray Keith, the second from George Constable, both friends of his youth; he had died in 1803, she in 1818.[36] The difference goes deeper than the likeness. As the study of an obsession, Elspat's tragedy might suit quite another sort of genius than Scott's; for the tragedy of Robin Oig M'Combich he is very well equipped.

Robin is one of that remarkable race of men who, recognizing the force of change, transformed themselves within a generation from cattle reivers to cattle drovers.[37] In the conduct of his life, he has come to terms with the present, and his pride in his own traditional past is a carefully guarded secret. His forbearance under provocation is deceptive: it

---

[33] Oldbuck's scepticism is manifestly his own.

[34] *Journal*, p. 150 (27 May 1826) and p. 168 (8 July 1826).

[35] Ballantyne had condemned 'The Two Drovers'. See *Journal*, p. 331 (22 July 1827).

[36] In the first edition he describes the stories as 'long meditated', I. xxvii; in the second (the 'Magnum') he explicitly owns his indebtedness (pp. xxxii and xxxiv). In a note to the former passage he gives the date of Mrs M. K.'s death as shortly before 1831—perhaps a symptom of his state of mind.

[37] See A. R. B. Haldane, *The Drove Roads of Scotland* (1952). Something of this piece of history is captured in *Rob Roy*, but lost in the romantic entanglements.

comes, not from a meek temper, but from a sense of his own worth and dignity, were he but in his own place. He knows that, once he crosses the Highland Line, he will be at a disadvantage, and is resolved not to be ruffled by slights from strangers. But, as in classical tragedy, human endeavours to avert foreseen disaster serve to bring it closer. Deprived of his dirk, he is unable to react immediately and directly to the intolerable affront, physical assault—a reaction which might have been foiled, or, failing that, condoned. The delayed response discloses his archaic, and, to southern judgement, vindictive code of honour, and he and the involuntary challenger are alike destroyed. The challenger, Harry Wakefield, is the stereotype of the stupid, well-meaning Englishman. Scott was often content to let one character give occasion to another's act or suffering, without manifesting more of himself than this function requires. What may be called propulsion is provided by the rascally bailiff, working on indifferent human material.

All this has to be conveyed in less than half the space taken by *The Highland Widow*—and of those few pages nearly one-fifth is given to the judge's charge to the jury at Carlisle. The narrative is indeed in Scott's 'bettermost manner'. He has so far forgotten his fictitious narrators as to designate 'a young lawyer'—that is, his friend George Constable who might well have been young when the actual tragedy played itself out—as its witness and reporter. But it is above all by means of the dialogue that Scott communicates that sense of an older world, out of which Robin comes to his doom. Upon the turmoil of departure he scatters a few Gaelic words, intimating that Robin and his aunt, with her fatal second sight, converse in their native tongue. Thereafter Robin will use it only to give safe vent to his opinion of the company in which he finds himself. He may be supposed sometimes to think in it, as when, knowing himself a dead man, he tells Morrison: ' "Ye winna meet with Robin Oig again either at tryste or fair." ' In the meantime, however, he is content to chaffer with Square Ireby in the dialect expected of him.[38] He

---

[38] Johnson had reported: 'Those Highlanders that can speak English commonly speak it well'; (*A Journey to the Western Islands of Scotland, Works*, Yale, IX. 36). Scott may witness to a later phase when,

scarcely rises above it when, trapped by mischance and goaded not only by enemies but even by his former friend, he expostulates: ' "If you think I have done you wrong, I'll go before your shudge, though I neither know his law nor his language." ' How then does he come to speak with simple grandeur at the end? Scott had achieved this when he gave Hamish MacTavish the words for a last message to his mother: ' "Tell her Hamish Bean is more glad to die than ever he was to rest after the longest day's hunting." ' But Hamish is speaking to the minister in his own tongue, translated without a flourish.

In what language is Robin Oig speaking, when, his archaic code of honour having compelled him to kill his friend, he casts the dirk onto the blazing hearth with the words ' "There, . . . take me who likes—and let fire cleanse blood if it can" '? Or when he replies to the expected sentence: ' "I give a life for the life I took", he said, "and what can I do more?" ' After many re-readings, I am not sure. Neither do I think that it matters. The two languages have mingled, like the waters of a tributary stream with those of a river, subtly changing the rhythm of the current for a brief while. And, whether Robin speaks Gaelic or a straightforward translation of his thoughts—that is, whether we are to imagine the speaker or the narrator translating—Scott is standing fast by his principle: simple people may command the language of passion at its proper height. But I would rather say: Scott himself was assured of the grandeur that can inhere in common life, and his instinct—so trustworthy when he surrendered to it—gave him the power to express this. So perhaps that gesture of fellowship with Wordsworth was not misdirected after all.

With Thackeray's language in *Esmond*, I leave for a while the advantages of a regional idiom, and the perils of an alien tongue, returning to the predicament of the story-teller who intends us to understand that his characters, who may include his imaginary narrator, use English, though of another age than ours. Provided he does not venture further back than the eighteenth century, his problem is definable, and therefore (in one way or another) soluble. Models of both written and spoken English are available; he must choose the

coming south by necessity, they had evolved a dialect to suit their needs.

best for his particular purpose. Authenticity is not all; the language he chooses must have the right associations for the common reader. If Thackeray had drawn for the language of *Esmond* on such sources as he used for its history and topography,[39] he might have earned considered esteem, but not spontaneous appreciation. True, those sources yield merely written English; but, even if he had had at his disposal such a treasury as *The Oxford Book of English Talk*,[40] he might well have demurred at its insistent strangeness for a modern ear. In turning to the *Tatler* and *Spectator*—notably the de Coverley papers—he could count on a pleasurable and sufficiently knowledgeable response from his contemporaries. Whether such an impression as they received would prove durable is another question.

I have suggested that the history of literary forgery and imposture may, despite all that separates these two from the acknowledged illusion of fiction, disclose one odd circumstance that they have in common.[41] An imposter's performance, no matter how plausible in his own day, will betray itself to future generations, even to those among them who are no better informed than their forebears. How a comparable change may come about in relation to a work of fiction is illustrated by *Esmond*.

Thackeray was not, of course, bent on deceiving his readers. What he did intend, and in his day achieve, has been set out, nowhere so well as in that Oxford edition of *The History of Henry Esmond* with commentary and notes by T. C. Snow and W. Snow.[42] Therefore I quote from that part of their introduction which is devoted to the style and language of the novel[43]—the more readily since this admirable edition is out of print and hard to obtain.

It is sometimes said that *Esmond* is written completely in the style of the early eighteenth century. Whether anybody could do such a thing, and whether it would be worth doing if any-

[39] See J. A. Sutherland, *Thackeray at Work* (1974), Appendix II, 'The Esmond Notebook'.
[40] ed. James Sutherland (1953).
[41] See p. 137, above.
[42] 1909; the general introduction by Saintsbury.
[43] This section occupies pp. xxvii to xxxii.

body could, are questions which may be left to themselves. It is certain that Thackeray did not do it. What he did was much more delightful. Partly by natural affinity with the age of Anne, and partly by the skilful use of its forms of speech at selected points, he created an illusion as if it was present throughout, while in fact he was allowing himself abundant material derived from the nineteenth century. Such an illusion does not impose on us when we test the language by analysis, but that is exactly what we are not meant to do, and what the ordinary human reader would not think of doing while he is enjoying the book.

This argument the editors substantiate, examining accidence and syntax, the use of eighteenth-century idiom and 'negative archaism . . . the avoidance of anything modern'; and they estimate the demands made by a range of thought and feeling not expressed in the *Tatler* and *Spectator*, observing moreover that the periodical essay affords no model for the give and take of conversation. For every point in this argument they give precise reference.

These two editors have no patience with the reader who spoils his own enjoyment of *Esmond* by fault-finding analysis. They do not allow however, for the ear which flinches instinctively at a false note. Seventy years have gone by since they wrote, and the likelihood of this reaction has grown. In trying to understand this we must reckon with these factors: in reading with proper attention—no more, no less—such a work as this, the mind's ear is naturally sensitive to three distinct voices: the voice of the age in which the author purports to be writing; the voice of the age in which he is writing; and his own voice. Clearly, the second of these, being part of their every-day experience, will be less noticeable to his contemporaries than it is to us; and this may be true of his own voice, familiar to them from habitual acquaintance with his other writings. Thackeray had a distinct voice, characterized by Geoffrey Tillotson as giving a peculiar sense of continuity to all his works: 'The most powerful of the agents making for continuity is, of course, prose style, and it is particularly powerful [in Thackeray's prose], because, unlike the style of Dickens and Henry James, it remained constant, or as near so as matters, throughout Thackeray's career.[44] We may therefore now be forgiven for questioning some turns of expression in *Esmond* which formerly passed muster.

Mindful of Johnson's 'poring fellow' who would dispute the barren state of an orchard by pointing to an apple and two pears, I do not mean to enumerate instances of word or phrase which satisfied Thackeray's contemporaries[45] but perturb us. I shall rather try to develop the admission of the two Oxford editors that between the content of *Esmond* and the mood of Thackeray's models there will sometimes be discrepancy. 'He was obliged . . . to think and feel as they could not have thought and felt.' Although thought and the language in which it is expressed cannot be entirely separated, they do succeed in singling out a romantic colouring in description, and what I may call an idiom of thought in 'disquisitions'—for example, on infelicity in marriage—which do not belong to the prose of Queen Anne's age. I offer the further suggestion that, in respect of this idiom of thought, one age differs from another in the way in which its writers relate general and particular. Which initiates, and which develops a theme? How are we led from one to the other? This is obviously too big a subject for handling in what can only be a mere parenthesis in another argument. I must be content to illustrate Thackeray's characteristic way of passing to and fro between general and particular with the help of apostrophe, by quoting passages from Esmond's visit to his mother's grave:

Esmond came to this spot in one sunny evening of spring, and saw, amidst a thousand black crosses, casting their shadows across the grassy mounds, that particular one which marked his mother's resting-place. Many more of those poor creatures that lay there had adopted that same name, with which sorrow had rebaptized her, and which fondly seemed to hint their individual story of love and grief. . . . Then came a sound of chanting, from the chapel of the sisters hard by; others had long since filled the place,which poor Mary Magdalene once had there, were kneeling at the same stall, and hearing the same hymns and prayers in which her stricken

---

[44] *Thackeray the Novelist* (1954), p. 50.

heart had found consolation. Might she sleep in peace; and we, too, when our struggles and pains are over! But the earth is the Lord's as the heaven is; we are alike His creatures here and yonder. . . . I felt as one who had been walking below the sea, and treading amidst the bones of shipwrecks.[46]

That could not have been written before the end of the eighteenth century at earliest. Set it beside many other, similar passages from *Esmond*, and the voice of the nineteenth century, and of Thackeray himself, is inescapable.

With Stevenson and Kipling I come round once again to the need for an invented idiom—by which I mean, in the first place, one for which there is no specific model in past literature. General influence is another matter. Any attempt to devise a prose style more stately and aloof than that of the writer's own age is likely to carry certain overtones—though this will cease to be true if the clergy continue to deny us the *sound* of the Authorized Version. But the particular need of these two story-tellers is for that sleight of pen by which they may persuade us that the people in their stories are speaking another language than that in which they themselves are writing: Urdu, Samoan—whatever the tale requires. While the spell works, we may even be half persuaded that we ourselves are listening to that other language. This performance is not of course an act of invention in the sense that belongs to the secret language which a family of children or a pair of lovers may invent, since it must be intelligible outside the magic circle. Indeed, if the story *matters*, it cannot afford even such nonce-words as Edward Lear makes up. Nevertheless, we may fairly call it a verbal artifact, and notice the evident enjoyment with which Stevenson and Kipling set about it. For *Kim*, Kipling had to devise means of persuading us that his characters were using several distinct Indian languages. In two of the Polynesian tales collected—contrary to his intention—in his *Island Nights Entertainments*, Stevenson had to persuade us that we were listening to islanders talking among themselves.[47] Unfortunately, these lie outside my field

[45] Mrs Tillotson has pointed out to me that their knowledge of eighteenth-century prose was far less than his.
[46] Book II, Chapter xiii.
[47] 'The Bottle Imp' and 'The Isle of Voices'. The first of these,

of scrutiny, alike as to place and time: whatever their association with the past for us, the characters in these tales, with the possible exception of the Lama, were not so distanced for their authors.

In the Puck books Kipling had to sustain a distinct and precarious linguistic illusion. What he achieved is a make-believe which holds, so long as it is implicit. Puck's inopportune joke, when he tells Parnesius of Dan's struggles with Latin grammar—' "The beauties of your native tongue, O Parnesius, have enthralled this young citizen" '[48]—tears the delicate web. Drawn into this make-believe, we have been taking it for granted that anyone who formerly lived in this island can speak with the children in their language, no matter what barriers time has raised between a British Roman, an Anglo-Saxon, or an Anglo-Norman and today's speech. Explicit reference to this assumption lays bare its fragility; but no strain is put upon it by St. Wilfrid's Latin benediction, or his reply, when Dan volunteers (of the *'Dies Irae'*) that it is in Latin: ' "There is no other tongue." '[49] The children have taken their own measures with the Latin inscription 'Orate p. annema . . .', calling that part of the church 'Panama corner'. Besides, the Saint is not speaking to them. For the same reason, it does not disturb their happy intercourse with Sir Richard Dalyngridge when he recalls that Witta, the 'sea thief' and explorer, ' "spoke a little in French, a little in South Saxon, and much in the Northman's tongue" '.[50] It is only the langage in which these tales are told to the children that must never be called in question.

One seemingly odd, but really quite natural, result is to be taken into account. It is not enough to assert that the language of Kipling's Romans, Saxons, Normans, and, in due course, English narrators is 'frankly modern'.[51] If the story-

---

though based on a Victorian melodrama, was intended for a Polynesian audience and for translation into Samoan. See the note prefixed to the tale and the letter to Colvin of 19 Mar. [1891]; *Letters*, Colvin, III. 249; from Vailima.

[48] *Puck of Pook's Hill*: 'A Centurion of the Thirtieth'.
[49] *Rewards and Fairies*: 'The Conversion of St. Wilfrid'.
[50] 'The Knights of the Joyous Venture'.
[51] G. M. Trevelyan, *A Layman's Love of Letters* p. 33.

tellers are compared over the range of both books, it will appear that, the further back they are set in time, the more 'frankly modern' their language. This is no mere paradox. A Roman centurion and an Anglo-Saxon archbishop cannot come half-way to meet us. A craftsman of Tudor England and a girl living under the Regency[52] can, though this may amount to little more than an occasional turn of phrase gathered from Elizabethan or late-eighteenth-century comedy. Midway between, Sir Richard Dalyngridge uses an idiom only slightly more archaic than I could have heard in childhood from my elders. Where the language of the period fails him, Kipling seeks that of the type. Parnesius speaks as a soldier— more specifically, a young officer. Is it going too far to say that the talk between St. Wilfrid and Meon recalls that of a Victorian country squire and his rector, supposing the churchman to be a dignitary in some sort of retirement?

Kipling's *collected*, as distinct from his *invented*, language has been censured, and is indeed too often open to question. I doubt whether any knowledgeable person would defend unreservedly the speech of his soldiers, and I offer no defence of his *ballad Scottish*. Perhaps he attempted too much, putting his tales into the mouths of too wide a variety of narrators. It is a pity that we cannot argue from the *Puck* stories, where the power of language to evoke the past is always in some degree limited by the proposed terms of the illusion.[53] Here he devises other means, building a world in which the visible and tangible predominate: people, places, things are charged with evocative power. Yet it should be remembered that even the least of these — things — may require nice command of words to convey their appearance and function to us. The mysterious *thing* brought on board by the Chinaman, to Sir Richard 'the wise iron', has to be depicted in words for Dan to recognise it as a compass.[54] Again, when the children need to imagine another sort of armour than that they see Sir Richard wearing, an excuse is found for bringing it to the

---

[52] 'The Wrong Thing' and 'Marklake Witches'.
[53] Even within those limits, Miss Tompkins is able to show what fine shades of linguistic difference distinguish the several Roman-British stories. See *The Art of Rudyard Kipling*, 1959, pp. 72-3.
[54] 'The Knights of the Joyous Venture'.
[55] 'Old Men at Pevensey'.

mind's eye: Fulke, Sir Richard recalls, 'was cased all in that new-fangled armour which we call lizard-mail. Not like my hauberk here . . . but little pieces of dagger-proof steel overlapping on stout leather. We stripped it off (no need to spoil good harness by wetting it), and in the neck-piece found the same folden piece of parchment which we had put back under the hearth-stone'.[55] So, in various and unobtrusive ways, means are found for establishing the story in a former age, without the hindrance of 'glossarial terms', which would disturb that illusion of distant events recounted to present-day hearers by someone who *was there*.

Words, however, do not merely tell us about things; they enlist them in the service of imagery. And so we come back to that initial problem: the writer's dependence on a range of allusion which he shares with his readers. But suppose the very images vanish from human consciousness? Living in a world which has changed out of recognition within the current century, I am bound to wonder how much of our older literature will be intelligible a generation hence. What will become of that potent image of desolation, the *cold hearth-stone*? Will it mean anything to town-dwellers? Will it mean much even to country-dwellers? Will it carry its whole burden of meaning except to those who have seen a deserted village? Perhaps the story-teller, less regarded but more approachable than the poet, may keep such symbols as this alive in the imagination.

[55] 'Old Men at Pevensey'.

Appendix

To relieve the foot-notes of a heavy load, I have reserved for this Appendix a summary account of authorities claiming for Shakespeare the authorship of that passage in the manuscript play, *Sir Thomas More*, which is known as *Addition D*.

The Book of Sir Thomas More, edited for the Malone Society by W. W. Greg (1911). The attribution is considered, but not unreservedly accepted.

E. Maunde Thompson, *Shakespeare's Handwriting* (1916).

Shakespeare's Hand in the Play of Sir Thomas More: Papers by A. W. Pollard, W. W. Greg, E. Maunde Thompson, J. Dover Wilson, and R. W. Chambers (1923). As the title implies, the contributors to this volume in the *Shakespeare Problems* series advance the claim severally, on various grounds and with varying degrees of confidence.

Therafter, the argument in favour of Shakespeare's authorship is developed in the following articles, and in books on Shakespeare and on More:-

W. W. Greg, 'Shakespeare's Hand Once More', in *The Times Literary Supplement* for 24 Nov. and 1 Dec. 1927; reprinted in *The Collected Papers of Sir Walter Greg*, ed. J. C. Maxwell (1966).

E. K. Chambers, *William Shakespeare, A Study of Facts and Problems* (1930).

Caroline Spurgeon, 'Imagery in the Sir Thomas More Fragment', in *The Review of English Studies*, VI (1930).

R. W. Chambers, *Sir Thomas More* (1935).

—— 'Shakespeare and the Play of More'; Lecture delivered 'in part' (1937); printed in *Man's Unconquerable Mind* (1939).

R. C.Bald, 'The Booke of Sir Thomas More and its Problems', in *Shakespeare Survey* (1949).

W. W. Greg, *The Shakespeare First Folio* (1955).

Harold Jenkins, A Supplement to Sir Walter Greg's edition of *Sir Thomas More*, in *Malone Society Collections*, VI (1961 1962)).

Furthermore, Peter Alexander printed the passage in his *William Shakespeare: The Complete Works* (1951).

Although the surviving evidence may be allowed to yield impressive probability rather than absolute certainty, it is manifest that the tide of opinion in this country for nearly half a century has been setting strongly and steadily towards belief.

Index